Success in the U.S.
Immigrants' True Stories

Connie Turner

Judy Shane

Janet Podnecky

OXFORD
UNIVERSITY PRESS

Oxford University Press
198 Madison Avenue
New York, NY 10016 USA

Great Clarendon Street
Oxford OX2 6DP England

Oxford New York

*Athens Auckland Bangkok Bogota Buenos Aires Calcutta
Cape Town Chennai Dar es Salaam Delhi Florence
Hong Kong Istanbul Karachi Kuala Lumpur Madrid
Melbourne Mexico City Mumbai Nairobi Paris São Paulo
Shanghai Singapore Taipei Tokyo Toronto Warsaw*

and associated companies in
Berlin Ibadan

OXFORD is a trademark of Oxford University Press.
ISBN 0-19-436154-3
Copyright © 2001 Oxford University Press

Library of Congress Cataloging-in-Publication Data

Turner, Connie, [DATE]
Success in the U.S. : immigrants' true stories /
Connie Turner, Judy Shane, and Janet Podnecky.
p. cm.
ISBN 0-19-436154-3
1. English language—Textbooks for foreign speakers. 2.
United States—Emigration and immigration—Problems,
exercises, etc. 3. Immigrants—United States—Problems,
exercises, etc. 4. Readers—Emigration and immigration. 5.
Readers—United States. 6. Readers—Immigrants. 7.
Readers—Success. I. Shane, Judy, [DATE] II. Podnecky,
Janet.
III. Title.

PE1128 .T87 2000
428.6'4—dc21   00-059858

No unauthorized photocopying.

Editorial Manager: Janet Aitchison
Senior Editor: Amy Cooper
Senior Production Editor: Robyn Clemente
Content Editor: Nan Clarke
Assistant Editor: Katharine Chandler
Design Manager: Lynne Torrey
Designer: Maj-Britt Hagsted and Mary Chandler
Art Buyer: Andrea Suffredini
Production Controller: Shanta Persaud
Printing (last digit): 10 9 8 7 6 5 4 3 2 1
Printed in Hong Kong.

Acknowledgments:
*Illustrations, realia, and maps by Gary Antonetti,
Maj-Britt Hagsted, Rita Lascaro, Patrick Merrell,
Vilma Ortiz-Dillon, and Gary Undercuffler
Photography by Connie Turner*

*The publisher would like to thank the following people for
their helpful reviews of the manuscript:*

*Lynda Calderwood, Shirley DuBois, Mary Hopkins,
Kathy Johnston, Julie Landau, Deborah Lazarus,
Cheryl Pavlik, Dian Perkins, Kay Powell, Jean Rose,
Mellanie Shepherd, Stephen Sloan, and Laura Webber*

The authors would like to thank:

*Amy, Nan, and Susan. They loved the people and accepted
the stories.*

Adele, Jack, Joyce, Kathy, and Sharon. They found the people.

*David, Maria, Perry, Sergio, Susanne, Yenework and Arij.
They are the people.*

Table of Contents

	Reading Skills	Writing Skills	SCANS Foundation Skills	SCANS Competencies
1 **David Tran** *Task:* How to Read a Recipe	**Comprehension** •Understand and interpret schedules and instructions •Sequence events •Follow directions •Recognize times •Use Abbreviations **Vocabulary** •Classify words **Decoding** •Short vowel (u) •Roots and suffixes	•Write a schedule •Write an order list	**Basic Skills** •Arithmetic: Perform computations •Speaking: Participate in conversation and discussion **Thinking Skills** •Knowing how to learn: Be aware of learning tools **Personal Qualities** •Self-Management: Assess skills	**Resources** •Allocate time to activities •Prepare schedules **Information** •Interpret and communicate information •Select information and communicate the results to others
2 **Suss Carlsson Cousins** *Task:* How to Pack and Ship	**Comprehension** •Understand and interpret abbreviations •Follow directions •Recognize key parts of labels and invoices **Vocabulary** •Classify words **Decoding** •Short vowel (i) •Suffix (-ing)	•Fill out an order form •Write a list of equipment	**Basic Skills** •Arithmetic: Perform computations •Speaking: Participate in conversation and discussion **Thinking Skills** •Solve problems **Personal Qualities** •Self-Management: Set personal goals	**Resources** •Allocate time and materials **Information** •Acquire and evaluate data **Technology** •Select equipment and tools
3 **Perecles Pappous** *Task:* How to Write a Meeting Memo	**Comprehension** •Understand and interpret want ads •Understand and interpret memos •Understand and interpret weekly meeting schedule •Recognize days and times **Vocabulary** •Classify words **Decoding** •Vowel diphthong (ɔ) •Word families	•Fill out a weekly appointment calendar •Write a memo	**Basic Skills** •Speaking: Participate in conversation and discussion **Thinking Skills** •Reason •Make decisions **Personal Qualities** •Sociability: Relate well to others	**Resources** •Allocate time, space, and staff **Interpersonal** •Lead and teach others **Information** •Communicate information **Systems** •Monitor and correct performance

	Reading Skills	Writing Skills	SCANS Foundation Skills	SCANS Competencies
4 **Lee Mei Bik** *Task:* How to Fill Out a Tax Form	**Comprehension** •Understand alphabetical order •Sequence events •Follow directions **Vocabulary** •Classify words **Decoding** •Vowel diphthong (oo) •Syllables	•Fill out forms: Record information accurately on tax forms •Write names for filing purposes (last name, first name)	**Basic Skills** •Arithmetic: Perform computations •Speaking: Participate in conversation and discussion **Thinking Skills** •Solve problems **Personal Qualities** •Self Esteem	**Information** •Organize files •Acquire and evaluate information
5 **Sergio Gonzalez** *Task:* How to Paint a Building	**Comprehension** •Understand and interpret schedules and instructions •Identify relevant details •Sequence events •Follow directions •Recognize times **Vocabulary** •Classify words **Decoding** •Consonant digraph (th)	•Write description of hazardous situation	**Basic Skills** •Arithmetic: Perform computations •Speaking: Participate in conversation and discussion **Thinking Skills** •Make decisions: Consider risks **Personal Qualities** •Responsibility: Pay attention to details	**Resources** •Allocate time to activities **Information** •Acquire and evaluate information •Interpret and communicate information **Systems** •Monitor and correct performance
6 **Yenework Alemayehu** *Task:* How to Use a Parenting Skill	**Comprehension** •Identify problems and suggest solutions •Sequence events **Vocabulary** •Use context clues **Decoding** •Initial consonant blends	•Write suggestions to help others	**Basic Skills** •Speaking: Participate in conversation and discussion **Thinking Skills** •Knowing how to learn: Be aware of community service directories **Personal Qualities** •Sociability: Respond appropriately; show politeness •Self Esteem	**Interpersonal** •Teach others •Work on a team •Serve customers **Information** •Interpret and communicate information

To the Teacher

Success in the U.S.: Immigrants' True Stories is a beginning level reading book for adult and young adult learners of English as a second language. This lively collection of six true stories about immigrants to the United States teaches both basic reading and workplace skills. *Success in the U.S.* is directly correlated to SCANS (Secretary's Commission on Achieving Necessary Skills), the U.S. government-recommended standards for workplace preparation. In *Success in the U.S.*, students have ample opportunity to develop and practice SCANS foundation skills, such as participating in conversation and discussion, making decisions, and solving problems, as well as SCANS competencies such as acquiring, interpreting, and communicating information and working as part of a team.

Each of the six chapters has three parts. Part 1 introduces the character and provides his or her story. The focus of the exercises in this part is on basic reading and SCANS foundation skills. Part 2 provides information about the character's typical workday, and exercises here promote the development of SCANS competencies. Part 3 contains a task that is typical of the character's profession and workplace. In this part exercises require the application of SCANS skills and competencies. Throughout the book, SCANS-related exercises are denoted by

The chapters do not need to be followed in order, but there is a gradual progression of linguistic complexity and task difficulty. Chapters 1–4 are written primarily in the simple present tense, while Chapters 5 and 6 are written in the simple past tense. As the book progresses, more modals are introduced and used. Vocabulary and sentence structure become increasingly more challenging. In the early chapters more factual information questions, asking *What? When?* and *Where?*, lay the foundation for later problem-solving and inference questions such as *Why?* and *How?* Activities in beginning chapters require single word or short phrase answers, which lead to more open-ended exercises in later chapters. Likewise, math skills progress from adding (or doubling) of numbers to more complex operations like multiplication. A wrap-up page at the end of each chapter encourages learners to make observations about the main character and express personal connections to the story. Most activities can be easily adapted for more advanced learners and/or multi-level classes.

The eclectic assortment of activities meets the diverse needs and learning styles of a broad range of learners. Theoretically, students do not need to be literate in their own languages, but some familiarity with the Roman alphabet is assumed, as well as some prior knowledge of basic survival English.

The material has been developed to support teaching approaches that include both phonics and whole language instruction. Suggested pre-reading activities (see General Teaching Notes, page vii) are designed to help pre-literate students with basic word recognition and word attack skills. New vocabulary is presented in boldfaced type and key words are depicted. Students are asked to make guesses and predictions, thereby activating and building background knowledge about each character and his/her workplace. These pre-reading activities are also important aids to students' understanding while they read.

Post-reading activities offer practice in a range of skills such as general comprehension, summarizing, sequencing, identifying cause and effect, and making inferences. Learners also practice discrete word attack skills such as sound-symbol correlation and structural analysis, along with more global skills such as categorizing words. Basic math skills in the context of word problems are also practiced.

Basic reading and writing skills and the targeted SCANS foundation skills and competencies in each chapter are listed in the Scope and Sequence on pages iv–v. Reading and writing are integrated, and activities often include listening and speaking as well, thereby allowing learners to use the information from the readings to communicate with each other about their own lives and experiences.

The General Teaching Notes are applicable to all of the chapters, and chapter-specific notes are on page 118. All of these are suggestions. We encourage you to use whatever techniques you think will best meet your students' individual needs and learning styles.

General Teaching Notes

Part 1: The Story

Pre-read

Classrooom piloting of *Success in the U.S.* clearly demonstrated how motivating it was for students to discover that each story in the book is a true one. Use the chapter opener picture to establish this fact and introduce the main character. Help learners pronounce his/her name. Identify the country of origin. Allow time for learners to look at photos and illustrations throughout the story. Encourage them to guess the person's occupation and to make predictions about the story.

To present vocabulary, have students scan the story for the boldfaced words and accompanying illustrations, and allow time for students to ask and answer questions about words they do not understand. Elicit additional vocabulary related to the person's occupation and workplace. Create a list or word web for chapter vocabulary and display it in the room or write the vocabulary words on word cards. Students can later use these cards for word games or spelling practice. The stories also lend themselves well to the use of realia to pre-teach other related vocabulary. *The Oxford Picture Dictionary* is another valuable resource for vocabulary presentation.

Read

We suggest that, initially, you read the entire *Part 1* story aloud to learners. Use actions, gestures, and even exaggerated expression to clarify meaning. Then have learners follow in their books as you reread the story to them, one paragraph at a time. Pause to focus on vocabulary and check comprehension using a variety of questions to encourage participation: *yes/no* questions, *or* questions, questions that require single word answers, and questions that require some critical thinking. You also might stop during the reading and allow volunteers to summarize what just happened and to guess or predict what might happen next.

After your vocalized reading, you may want to use shared reading, guided reading, and/or individual reading. For shared reading, have learners form pairs or small groups and read the story (or parts of the story). For guided reading, you can provide students with specific questions to answer as they read. You can also create a story map or flow chart to highlight major events; later, use the story map to guide learners as they retell or summarize parts of the story. Encourage them to compare the character's

experiences with their own. Learners can record their observations on a chart. Although individual reading requires no specific guidance prior to reading, you may want to establish a specific purpose before students begin to read. For example, ask students to read in order to find the answer to a general question or to obtain specific information about the character.

Post-reading

Student Book exercises

Make sure learners understand the directions. You can demonstrate by completing the first items on the board or an overhead transparency. Learners can work on these activities individually or in pairs. Go over the answers with the group or have students check their answers with each other in pairs or small groups.

Vocabulary reinforcement

Vocabulary is naturally reinforced as learners complete real-life speaking and writing tasks that require them to use the words they have encountered in the readings. For further reinforcement, prepare a set of word cards and picture cards and have learners practice matching the words and pictures. If learners enjoy drawing, use a drawing game. Ask volunteers to draw pictures of the vocabulary words for individuals or teams to guess.

Part 2: The Workday

Preview the vocabulary, and then present the reading selection as suggested for Part 1. Have students complete the exercises. You can use a chart or graphic organizer to summarize information in categories such as time, tasks, places, people, or tools used by the character.

Part 3: The Task

To introduce the vocabulary, you may want to use a Total Physical Response activity. In a typical Total Physical Response activity, the teacher first performs the actions while giving appropriate verbal cues or instructions. Then s/he gives the verbal cues and has learners perform the actions. Finally, one student gives the cues or commands and the others perform the actions.

Chapter Wrap-up

The wrap-up questions encourage students to form and express opinions and to apply what they have read about the characters to their personal experience. Have students complete the questions and share their answers. Invite discussion by asking questions like: *Would you like his or her job? Why or why not? How is your experience similar or different? What problems are in the story? What are the solutions? What makes this character successful?*

Additional Activities

• Have the class create a booklet; each learner can choose something about the character to write about and illustrate. To provide practice in sequencing and logical ordering, have students assemble the individual pages.

• Have learners write or share instructions for performing a task related to the occupation featured in the chapter.

• Ask learners to dramatize scenes from the story, create their own dialogs, or prepare role plays. Encourage them to use vocabulary from the chapter.

• Have students use *The Oxford Picture Dictionary* to write or talk about vocabulary specific to their own jobs and interests.

• Help students write a letter to the authors with their questions about the characters, in care of:

Oxford University Press
American English Language Teaching Division
198 Madison Avenue
New York, New York, 10016

This can also be done as part of the *Success Stories Wrap-up*.

Success Stories Wrap-up

The photographs on the front cover can be used for a culminating activity after each chapter or at the end of the book.

For low-beginning learners, this can be a whole class activity. Ask learners to look at a picture that you or they select. Elicit sentences about the chapter related to that picture. Ask questions to guide the group. Have a volunteer write the sentences on the board or on a large piece of paper as learners make suggestions. Then help the group determine the logical sequence of the sentences to create the story. Learners can copy the story for themselves and then read it aloud to a partner or read it together as a whole class.

More advanced learners can do the activity in groups or in pairs. Encourage learners to share their stories with the rest of the class.

To the Teacher

Chapter 1

David Tran

Where does David work?
What does he do?

1   My name is Hung Tran.
I am from **Vietnam.**

2   Americans call me David.
David is easy for American
people to pronounce.

3   In Vietnam I fixed TVs.
I need work here.
I look at TV repair books.
The vocabulary is very difficult.
I say, "Oh, no!"

4 I go to a sewing **factory.**
   I put **buttons** and
   buttonholes on shirts.

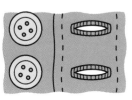

   I make 30 cents on shirts
   with 30 buttons.
   I make no **money** on shirts
   with no buttons.

   I say, "Oh, no!"
   I need a new job.

5 I like **food.**
   I go to a restaurant.
   I wash and cut
   vegetables.
   I am a cook's helper.
   The cook makes mistakes.
   Everybody gets **angry.**

   I say, "Oh, no!"
   I need a new job.

6   My brother, Ken, is a **baker.**
He bakes **bread.**
I say, "Please give me a job."
He says, "OK."
I work very hard.
I am a baker's helper.

7   The **bakery** is dirty.
The equipment is broken.
Ken doesn't like the bakery.
He says, "I quit."
I say, "Oh, no!"

8   Ken has a **partner.**
His partner says, "Oh, no!
Now I need another baker."

9   I say, "I want to be a baker."
He says, "You work hard.
Do you want to be my partner?"
I say, "OK."

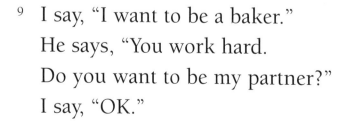

10 I go home and read a cookbook.
I multiply the recipe by eight
for the bakery.
My bread tastes like **wood.**
It's not good.
I say, "Oh, no!"

11 I make bread again and again.
I use good ingredients.
Good **flour.** Good **butter.**
I mix everything well.
I check the **temperature**
of the **dough.**

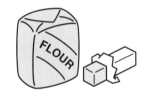

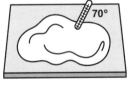

12 Now my **customers**
buy my bread.
They like it and I am **happy.**

13 You want to be a baker?
You can't be lazy.
You have to work hard.
Working hard is most important.
You need good **luck** too.

14 Three years ago
I was a baker's helper.
Now I have a **family**,
a car, a **house**,
and a business.
I think I am a lucky and
successful person.

Exercise A Circle *True* or *False*.

1. David fixed TVs in Vietnam.   (True)   False
2. Now David lives in Vietnam.   True   False
3. He sewed buttons on shirts in a factory.   True   False
4. He was a cook's helper in a restaurant.   True   False
5. Now David is a baker.   True   False
6. David works in a factory now.   True   False
7. David has a house.   True   False
8. David says, "Be lazy."   True   False

Exercise B Answer the questions.

Before

Now

1. Where did David work before?

   He worked in a ___factory___.

2. Where does David work now?

   Now he works in a _____.

3. Where did you work before?

   I worked _____.

4. Where do you work now?

   Now I work _____.

Exercise C Look at the story again. Write the skills David needs for the jobs.

Name: David Tran	
Job	**Skills**
baker	1. <u>read a cookbook</u> 2. _____ 3. _____
cook's helper	4. _____ 5. _____
factory worker	6. _____ 7. _____

Exercise D Fill in your name. Write jobs you had or want. Write the skills you need for these jobs.

Name:	
Job	**Skills**
	1. _____ 2. _____ 3. _____
	4. _____ 5. _____ 6. _____
	7. _____ 8. _____ 9. _____

Study the words in the box. Complete the sentences with the correct words.

> bake + er = **baker**   bake + ery = **bakery**
>
> bake + s = **bakes**   bake + ed = **baked**

1. David works in a _____ <u>bakery</u> _____ .
2. David is a _____ .
3. David _____ bread yesterday.
4. David _____ good bread now.

Write the food words and the feelings words.

> bread   angry   vegetables   lazy
>
> butter   cream   happy   lucky

Food	**Feelings**
<u>bread</u>	_____
_____	_____
_____	_____
_____	_____

Listen to the sound of *u* in *up* and *but*. Write other words with the same sound.

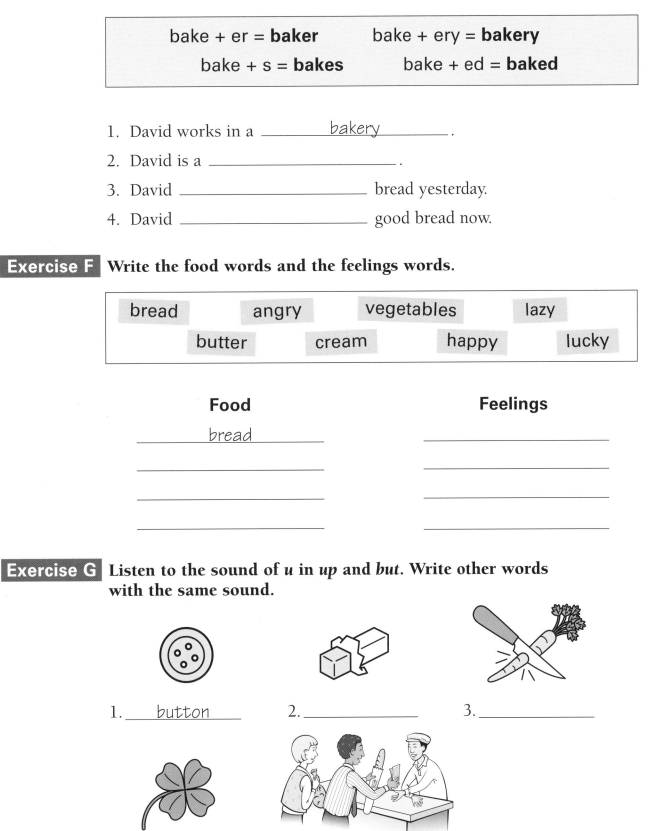

1. <u>button</u>   2. _____   3. _____

4. _____   5. _____

1   I work six days a week.
    I get up at 3:00 in the morning.
    I go to the bakery at 3:30.

2   First I bake **muffins**
    and **croissants.**
    People eat muffins
    and croissants for breakfast.

3   After that I bake bread
    and **cookies.** I finish
    baking at 2:00 in the afternoon.

4   I am **tired.**
    I sleep in my car for two hours.

5   I mix muffin and bread dough
     for the next day.
     For example, on Sunday
     I mix the dough to bake
     on Monday morning.

6   I hire **employees.**
     I train employees to help customers.
     I **pay** employees.

7   I **count** the money.
     My partner counts the money.

8   I go home at 8:00 or 9:00 at night.
     I am very tired.

9   My customers are happy.
     I am happy.

Write the times and what David does.

goes to the bakery   sleeps   goes home   gets up

David's Schedule	
Time	What does David do?
in the morning at 3:00	He _____gets up_____ .
_____	He _____ .
in the afternoon at _____	He _____ .
at night at _____	He _____ .

Ask a partner about David's day.

Examples: *What does David do at 3:00 in the morning?*

When does David go home?

Exercise B Write the times and what you do. Draw hands on the clocks to show the times.

My Schedule	
Time	What do you do?
in the morning at (clock) _____	 I _____ _get up_ _____ .
  (clock) _____	 I _____ .
in the afternoon at (clock) _____	 I _____ .
  (clock) _____	 I _____ .

Continue your schedule on the next page.

My Schedule

Time	What do you do?
at night at _____	I _____.
   _____	I _____.

Ask a partner about his or her schedule.

Examples: *What do you do at 7:00 in the morning?*
When do you study?

<u>Ingredients</u>

1 pound butter

1 pound **brown sugar**

10 ounces creamy **peanut butter**

3 1/2 cups all-purpose flour

1/4 teaspoon **baking powder**

1/4 teaspoon **baking soda**

1/2 teaspoon **salt**

1 cup **peanuts**

<u>Directions for Making Cookies</u>

1. Preheat oven to 350°.

2. Mix butter, brown sugar, and peanut butter in a bowl.

3. Combine flour, baking powder, baking soda, and salt in a different bowl.

4. Add flour mixture to butter mixture. Mix about two minutes.

5. Chop peanuts. Add peanuts to cookie dough.

6. Use a small ice-cream scoop to drop the dough onto the cookie sheet.

7. Bake 10 to 12 minutes. When you see cracks in the cookies, they're ready!

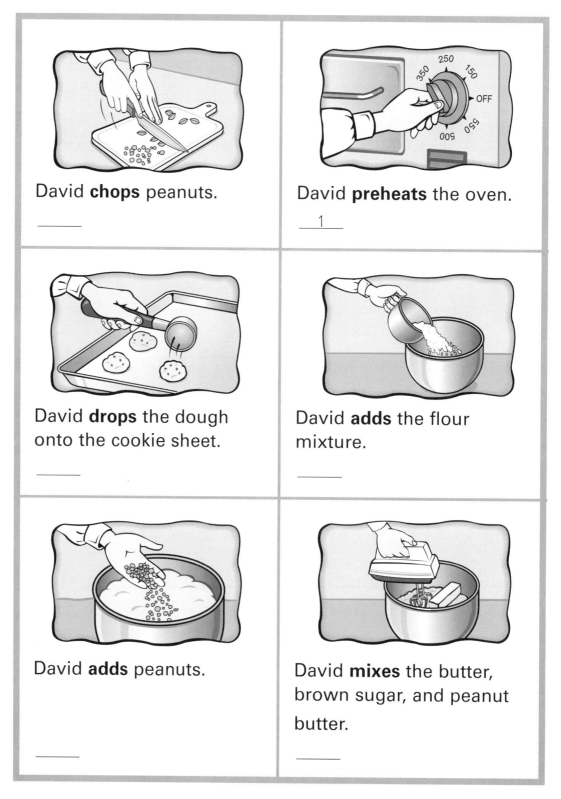

David **chops** peanuts.

_____

David **preheats** the oven.

1

David **drops** the dough onto the cookie sheet.

_____

David **adds** the flour mixture.

_____

David **adds** peanuts.

_____

David **mixes** the butter, brown sugar, and peanut butter.

_____

Ask a partner about the recipe.

Examples: _What does David do first?_

What does he do after that?

Look again at the directions for making cookies on page 15.
Write the correct words from the box under the pictures.

mix   drop   chop   bake   preheat   add

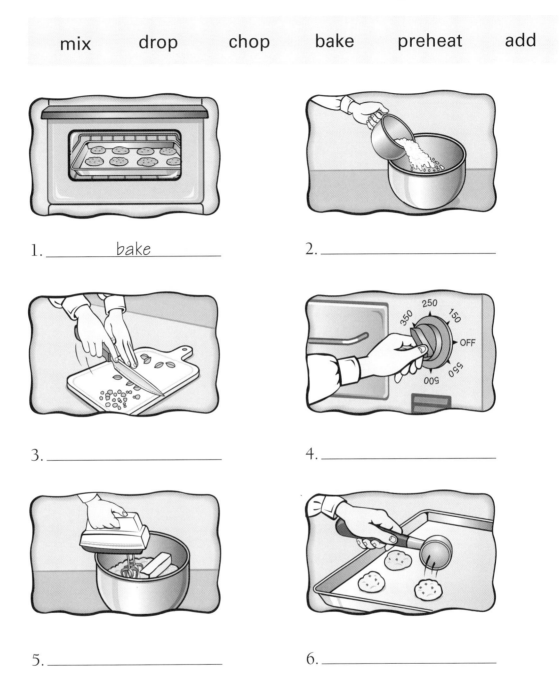

1. _____bake_____   2. _____

3. _____   4. _____

5. _____   6. _____

Weights and Measurements		Abbreviations
ounce		oz
pound		lb
cup		c
teaspoon		tsp

Exercise C Look at the chart above. Then write the abbreviations and the ingredients on the lines.

1 pound butter   *1 lb butter*

1 pound brown sugar   _____

10 ounces peanut butter   _____

3 1/2 cups flour   _____

1/4 teaspoon baking powder   _____

1/4 teaspoon baking soda   _____

1/2 teaspoon salt   _____

1 cup peanuts   _____

Talk about the ingredients with a partner.

Example: Student A: *I need butter.*

Student B: *How much butter?*

Student A: *One pound.*

Exercise D David wants to make two batches of cookies.
Make a shopping list for him.

1 Batch of Cookies

1 lb butter

1 lb brown sugar

10 oz peanut butter

3 1/2 c flour

1/4 tsp baking powder

1/4 tsp baking soda

1/2 tsp salt

1 c peanuts

2 Batches of Cookies

2 lb butter

_____

_____

_____

_____

_____

_____

_____

Exercise E Think of a recipe you like. Write the ingredients.
Then write the weights and measurements you need.

My Recipe for _____

Ingredients	Weights and Measurements

Tell a partner about the ingredients you need.

1. David says, "I think I am a lucky and successful person."

   What do you think?
   Circle the words.

a. David is successful because he

   is angry.   can fix TVs.   works hard.   makes mistakes.

   is not lazy.   is lazy.   can bake bread.

b. David is successful because he has

   a family.   a car.   a business.   a job.   a repair book.

   a house.   a TV.   a restaurant.

2. What can you do to be successful in the United States?

   _____

   _____

3. What will you have when you are successful in the United States?

   _____

   _____

4. Write a question for David.

   _____

   _____

Chapter 2

Suss Carlsson Cousins

Where does Suss work?

What does she make?

1   I came to **Manhattan** in 1982.
    I came on New Year's Eve.
    It was a beautiful evening,
    and I fell in love with Manhattan
    that night.

2   I had a clothing store
    and a **boyfriend** in **Sweden.**
    I left everything.

3   I have a tourist **visa.**
    After six months
    I go back to Sweden
    to renew my visa.
    I don't want to do this
    every six months.
    I want to stay in America.

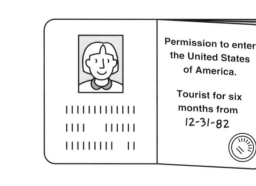

Permission to enter
the United States
of America.

Tourist for six
months from
12-31-82

4 Then I meet a guy
and **fall in love**.
He gets down on his **knees**
and proposes.
Six weeks after that we **get married**.

5 We need money.
I **knit** and take my **sweaters** to stores.
I sell one here and one there.

6 I work in a restaurant for money.
I take classes to learn the **hand loom**.

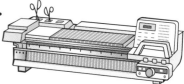

7 One day I call the Bill Cosby TV show.
I say, "I make handmade sweaters.
Are you interested?"

8 A **limousine** picks me up
in my run-down **neighborhood**.
I start making one-of-a-kind
sweaters for Bill Cosby.

9 My husband is an **actor**.
He gets work on soap operas.
I make sweaters for soap opera people.

10 After five years we decide to have a baby.
It's not easy to have **children**
in New York City.
My husband wants to be in movies.
We move to Los Angeles.

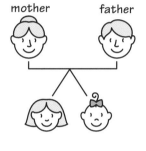

11 I make sweaters for my baby **daughter**.
I take pictures
of 12 different sweaters to a store.
The store orders 10 of each.
I don't think I can do it.
I **cry** and knit. I knit and cry.
But I am going to finish!

12 I rent a house with a **garage**
for more space.
I get big orders.
I say to my husband,
"We need a bigger house."

13 Now I make and sell **clothes**
    and teach knitting classes.
    Many Americans don't know
    how to knit.

14 Knitting is my passion.
    I get ideas
    from museums and buildings.
    I look at people.
    I put all my colors together.
    With a **string** I make any shape I want.
    I think that is lovely.

15 I make sweaters for famous
    athletes and actors.
    It's a long **list.**

16 I was not a businesswoman.
I am now!
You learn and you grow.

17 I am building this business for my children.
I'm successful because I don't give up.
I work hard. I have a dream.
Sometimes I have problems,
but I don't stop.
I think, "How can I solve this problem?"

Circle *True* or *False*.

1. Suss came to Sweden in 1982.	True	(False)
2. She had a restaurant in Sweden.	True	False
3. Suss renews her visa every four months.	True	False
4. Suss knits sweaters.	True	False
5. Her husband is an actor.	True	False
6. They move to Los Angeles because her husband wants to be in movies.	True	False
7. Many stores and people like her sweaters.	True	False
8. Suss is building the business for her friend.	True	False

Exercise B **Answer the questions.**

1. When did Suss come to Manhattan?

   She came in _____ 1982 _____ .

2. Her husband wanted to be in movies. Where did they move?

   They moved to _____ .

3. When did you come to the United States?

   I came in _____ .

4. Where did you move?

   I moved to _____ .

Look at the story again. Write the missing numbers.

"I make sweaters for my baby daughter. I take pictures of

_____ different sweaters to a store. The store orders

_____ of each."

**Exercise D** Look at your answers in Exercise C. Now read the problems below. Find the answers in the box.

10	20	38	80	120

1. How many sweaters does Suss need to make altogether?

_____120_____

2. Suss knits. Now she has 40 sweaters. How many more does she need to make?

_____

3. Suss knits some more. Now she has 82 sweaters. How many more does she need to make?

_____

4. Suss makes 2 sweaters in 1 day. How many sweaters can she make in 5 days?

_____

5. How many sweaters can she make in 10 days?

_____

Now work with a partner. Write a problem about Suss and her sweaters. Find the answer. Give the problem to a new partner. Does your new partner get the same answer?

_____

_____

_____

Exercise E Study the words in the box. Complete the sentences
with the correct words.

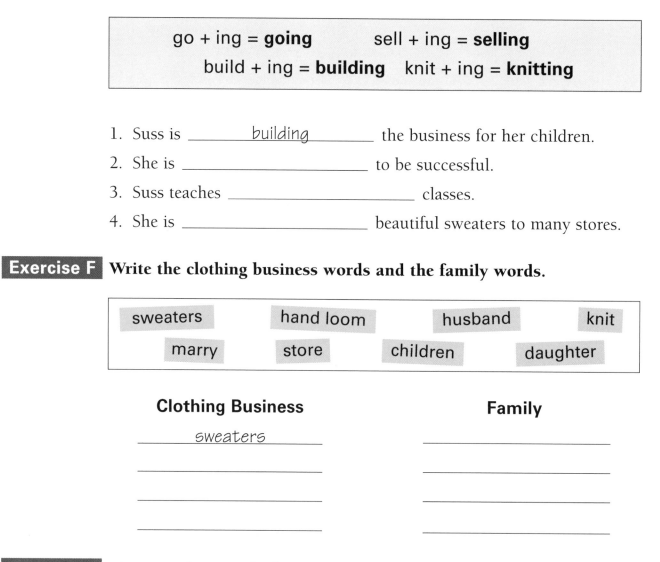

go + ing = **going**   sell + ing = **selling**

build + ing = **building**   knit + ing = **knitting**

1. Suss is _____building_____ the business for her children.

2. She is _____ to be successful.

3. Suss teaches _____ classes.

4. She is _____ beautiful sweaters to many stores.

Exercise F Write the clothing business words and the family words.

| sweaters | hand loom | husband | knit |
| marry | store | children | daughter |

Clothing Business

_____sweaters_____

_____

_____

_____

Family

_____

_____

_____

_____

Exercise G Listen to the sound of *i* in *it*. Say the words below. Check (✓) the
words that have the same sound.

1. __✓__ knit

2. _____ people

3. _____ visa

4. _____ teach

5. _____ meet

6. _____ bigger

7. _____ this

8. _____ list

1   I get up at 6:00 A.M. with my baby.
We play.
I have **coffee**
and think about what I'm going to do.

2   At 8:10 I take my **older** daughter
to school.
Then I go to work.
The store opens at 10:00.

3   I call everybody.
I pick colors, send faxes,
make appointments.
Time flies.
I eat lunch at work.

4   I am the **boss,**
    but I work with my employees.
    I knit, I **sew,** I **steam.**
    I pack and ship.

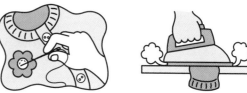

5   We close the store at 7:00 P.M.
    I go home.

6   My husband makes dinner,
    or we make dinner together.
    I put my kids to bed at 9:00.
    Then I read fashion **magazines**
    and go to bed.

7   Before I go to sleep
    I make a long list
    of everything
    I want to do.

Things Suss Does   **Machines She Uses**

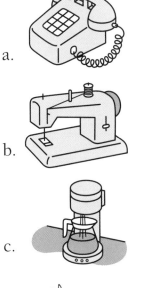

___c___ 1. makes coffee   a.

_____ 2. takes her daughter to school   b.

_____ 3. sends a fax   c.

_____ 4. calls everybody   d.

_____ 5. sews   e.

_____ 6. knits   f.

Ask a partner about Suss.

Examples: *What does Suss use to make coffee?*
What does she use to knit?

Exercise B Write the things you do with machines. Write the names or draw pictures of the machines.

Things I Do	Machines I Use

Ask a partner about what he or she does.

Examples: *What do you do?*

What do you use to _____ ?

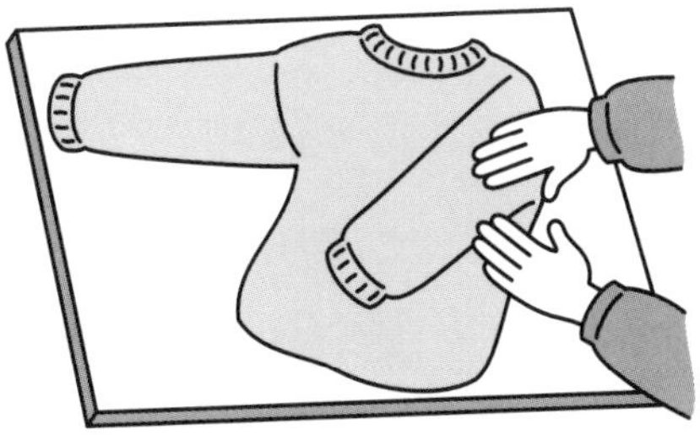

1 Steam and **fold** a sweater.

2 Look at the sweater order.
   Check the **style number.**
   Check the **size.**
   Check the **color.**

ORDER FORM

Style Number: 11768

Size: Small

Color: Red and White

3 Put the sweater
   in a plastic bag.
   Tape the bag closed.

4   Stamp a **padded envelope**
    with the **shipping number.**
    Stamp the padded envelope
    with the **return address.**
    Put the **packing slip pouch**
    on the envelope.

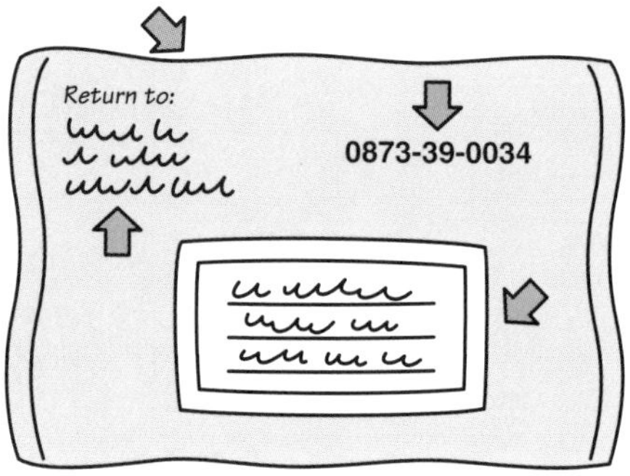

Return to:

0873-39-0034

5   Put the **invoice** inside.
    Put the sweater inside.
    Staple the envelope closed.
    Take the package to
    the shipping office.

Invoice

1 Sweater, Style # 11768

Size: Small

Color: Red and White

Price: $100

Look again at "How to Pack and Ship." Write the correct words from the box under the pictures.

style number   size   color   envelope

return address   invoice

Invoice

1 Sweater, Style # 11768

Size: Small

Color: Red and White

Price: $100

Return to:

Debbie Smith

150 Elm Street

Big City, NY

1. _____invoice_____

2. _____

Suss's Sweaters

4. _____ : Red and White

5. _____ : 11768

6. _____ : Small

3. _____

Look at the sweater orders. Match the hangtags with the orders.

_c_ 1.

Order #: D3566

Name: Joan Richards

Address: 339 South Park Street
Smalltown, IL 60000

Phone: (100) 555-8834

Size: S, (M,) L, XL

Style #: 7221D

Color: Brown

a.

S
Style 5335L
Hand wash.
$14.50

___ 2.

Order #: D3567

Name: Robert Fuentes

Address: 89 Maple Dr.
Topstown, MA 01991

Phone: (200) 555-3662

Size: S, M, (L,) XL

Style #: 5611P

Color: Blue

b.

XL
Style 1227D
Hand wash.
$22.95

___ 3.

Order #: D3568

Name: Tommy Sammis

Address: 212 Holmes St., Apt. 12
Bakertown, CA 91234

Phone: (300) 555-4387

Size: S, M, L, (XL)

Style #: 1227D

Color: Green

c.

M
Style 7221D
Hand wash.
$16.95

___ 4.

Order #: D3569

Name: Ivan Petrovich

Address: 442 Westwood Lane
Olwerk, NJ 07123

Phone: (400) 555-9023

Size: (S,) M, L, XL

Style #: 5335L

Color: White

d.

L
Style 5611P
Hand wash.
$12.50

Exercise C Fill out the order form for yourself.

Order Form

Date: _____

Customer Name: _____

Address: _____

_____

Phone #: _____

Sweater Order

Style Number: _____

Size:	S	M	L	XL
Color:	Blue	Red	Green	White
	Brown	Purple	Gray	Yellow
	Orange	Black		

Exercise D Ask a partner for the information in the order form below. Fill out the order form for your partner.

Order Form

Date: _____

Customer Name: _____

Address: _____

_____

Phone #: _____

Sweater Order

Style Number: _____

Size:	S	M	L	XL
Color:	Blue	Red	Green	White
	Brown	Purple	Gray	Yellow
	Orange	Black		

1. What were some of Suss's problems? What do you think?
   Circle the words.

   visa   no money   too many orders   house too small

              lazy   sick

2. What does Suss want for her children?

   _____

   _____

3. What do you want?

   _____

   _____

4. Write a question for Suss.

   _____

   _____

Chapter 3

Perecles Pappous

Where does Perecles work?
What does he do?

1 My name is Perecles Pappous.
I am from **Greece.**
Americans call me Perry.

2 Americans say, "Hello, Gary."
I think they say "Perry."
I say, "Hello."
They say, "Hi, Terry. Hi, Larry."
I say, "Hi! Hi!"
I think, "I need to **study** English."

3 People from my country tell me,
"Greek immigrants
own restaurants."
I say, "No. I am going to **school.**
I want to be a **professor.**"

4 But Greek people can help me.
  I see a Greek restaurant.
  I ask, "Can I work here?"
  They say, "You can be a **busboy**."

5 My boss says,
  "Professor! Clean the **table**."
  Customers say,
  "Professor! Bring us coffee."

6 I **graduate** from school.
  But now I do not want to be
  a professor.

7 I get a job in a **furniture** store.
  My job is inventory control.
  I count **chairs** and tables.
  This is not what I want.

8   I think.

American law is good.

In America the law is for the people.

I say, "I can go to law school.

I can study laws that help
employees.

I can study laws that help
employers also."

9   Five years later I am a lawyer in America.

I want to work for a big company.

Only small companies call me.

I say, "Well, I can begin small."

10 One day my boss is **sad.**
He says, "Your work is very good.
But the company
has no more money."
Now I don't have a job.
I am **scared.**

11 I know some lawyers.
I call them on the telephone.
I say, "I need a job."
I look in **newspapers.**
I make appointments.
I fill out **applications.**

Application for Employment

Name: _____

Address: _____

Job Desired: _____

Experience: _____

12 I find a job!
This company is not big,
but it is not small.
I like the work. I like the people.

13 Then I learn bad news.
This company does not make
money either.
Now I **worry.**

14 I say, "I have to look for
a better job."
I leave work at lunch time.
But I don't eat.
I have **interviews.**

15 One interview is with a big company.
They say, "You know the law.
You are good with people too."

16 Now I am a lawyer
   in a very big company.
   I say, "This is the law.
   That is the law."
   I help employees be successful.
   I help the company be successful.
   So I am successful too.

17 You can start anywhere.
   Learn everything you can.
   Help other people.
   I think these are the laws
   of success.

Circle *True* or *False*.

1. Perry wanted to have a restaurant.   True   (False)

2. Perry graduated.   True   False

3. He counted chairs and tables in a restaurant.   True   False

4. He went to law school.   True   False

5. Perry looked in newspapers for a school.   True   False

6. Perry works in a small company now.   True   False

7. He doesn't help other people.   True   False

8. Perry says, "Learn everything you can."   True   False

Exercise B **Answer the questions.**

1. What do you study at school?

   I study _____.

2. How can you look for jobs?

   I can _____.

Look at these ads from the newspaper. What are the jobs? Circle them.

a.

Help needed: Large, busy restaurant needs busboy. Part-time, evenings, and weekends. For application, see Leo at 675 Main Street.

b.

Full-time opening: Small law office needs qualified lawyer. Call 555-4321 for information or send résumé to M. Burke, 333 Center Rd., Manchester.

c.

Inventory control manager. Great starting position in big department store. No experience needed. Call 555-2524 for application and interview.

Exercise D Circle the letters of the ads that give answers to the questions. Some questions have two answers.

1. Which job is in a small company?   a   (b)   c

2. Which job is in a large company?   a   b   c

3. Which job do you need an application for? a   b   c

4. Which job do you need an interview for?   a   b   c

5. Which job can you call about information? a   b   c

Exercise E Write an ad for a job you had or want.

Help wanted: _____

_____

_____

_____

_____

_____

Exercise F   Study the words in the box. Complete the sentences with the correct words.

law	law + school = **law school**
law + s = **laws**	law + (y)er = **lawyer**

1. Perry works in a big company. He is a _____ lawyer _____ .
2. He went to _____ to study.
3. Perry says, "This is the _____ ."
4. "I can study _____ that help employees."

Exercise G   Write the school words and the job words. Some words can be both.

study	company	learn	professor
interview	employers	graduate	employees

School

_____ study _____

_____

_____

_____

Job

_____

_____

_____

_____

Exercise H   Listen to the sound of *a* in *all*. Say these words. Circle the letters that make the same sound.

1. c(a)ll
2. small
3. coffee
4. law
5. also

1 I have a **wife**
   and three daughters.
   We get up at 6:30 A.M.
   At 8:00 I go to my **office.**

2 My assistant says, "You have
   a **meeting** at 9:00.
   Can you have a second
   meeting at **noon**?"
   I say, "Yes, that's fine."

3 My first meeting is too long.
   I say, "Excuse me. I have
   a meeting at noon."
   My boss asks,
   "Is that meeting important?"
   I say, "Yes, it's very important."

4   I go to my second meeting.
    A manager says, "**Pregnant** women
    can't do their jobs."
    An employee says, "But
    they need their jobs."
    I say, "It's the law.
    We have to give pregnant women
    jobs they can do."

5   From 2:30 to 5:30 I **read**
    new laws. Then I write **memos.**
    At 7:00 I go home for dinner.

MEMO

To: All Employees
From: Perry Pappous
Date: March 12
Re: Staff meeting

We will meet today at 11:00 A.M. in t

6   At 8:00 my wife says, "Girls,
    it's time for **bed.**"
    They say, "Do we have to?"

7   I say, "It's the law."
    We **laugh.**

	Monday	Tuesday	Wednesday	Thursday	Friday
8:00 A.M.				meeting	
9:00			meeting		
10:00		meeting			meeting
11:00	meeting				
12:00 P.M.			meeting		
1:00					meeting
2:00	meeting				
3:00					

Circle the answers to the questions.

1. Perry has a meeting at 9:00 A.M. and 12:00 P.M. What day is it?

   a. Monday   b. Wednesday   c. Thursday

2. Perry has a meeting at 10:00 in the morning and 1:00 in the afternoon. What day is it?

   a. Tuesday   b. Monday   c. Friday

3. What time does Perry have a meeting on Tuesday?

   a. 10:00 A.M.   b. 10:00 P.M.   c. 2:00 P.M.

4. What time does Perry have a meeting on Thursday?

   a. 8:00 A.M.   b. 1:00 P.M.   c. 10:00 A.M.

5. How many meetings does Perry have on Monday?

   a. 1   b. 2   c. 3

Ask a partner about Perry's meetings.

Examples: *Does Perry have a meeting at 10:00 on Friday morning?*
When does Perry have a meeting on Monday?

Exercise B Write the meetings and appointments you have this week.

MY SCHEDULE					
	Monday	**Tuesday**	**Wednesday**	**Thursday**	**Friday**
8:00 A.M.					
9:00					
10:00					
11:00					
12:00 P.M.					
1:00					
2:00					
3:00					
4:00					
5:00					
6:00					
7:00					
8:00					
9:00					

Ask a partner about his or her schedule. Set a time for two meetings.

Example: Student A: *Can you have a meeting on Monday at 5:00 P.M.?*

Student B: *No, I can't. Can you have a meeting on Monday at 6:00 P.M.?*

Student A: *Yes, I can. Can you have a meeting on…?*

MEMO

To: All Employees
From: Perry Pappous
Date: March 12
Re: Staff meeting

We will meet today at 11:00 A.M. in the conference room.
This is the agenda:

1. Report: "How to Hire Good Employees"
2. Report: "How to Help Employees Work Better"
3. Discussion: Employee benefits
    a. medical insurance
    b. leave of absence
    c. holiday pay
    d. **vacation**
4. Review anti-discrimination laws
5. Other items

Please give me a copy of your report.

June

SUNDAY	MONDAY	TUESDAY	WEDNESDAY	THURSDAY	FRIDAY	SATURDAY
				1	2	3
4	5	6	7	8	9	10
11	12	13	14	15	16	17
18	19	20	21	22	23	24
25	26	27	28	29	30	

Exercise A **Look again at Perry's memo. Match the questions and answers.**

_e_ 1. What time is the meeting?   a. two

___ 2. Where is the meeting?   b. the employees

___ 3. Who is coming to the meeting?   c. in the conference room

___ 4. How many reports are there?   d. Perry Pappous

___ 5. What are employee benefits?   e. 11:00 A.M.

___ 6. Who needs copies of the reports?   f. medical insurance,
                                                  holiday pay, leave of
                                                  absence, vacation

Exercise B Read the sentences below. Which report are they from? Write *a* for "How to Hire Good Employees." Write *b* for "How to Help Employees Work Better."

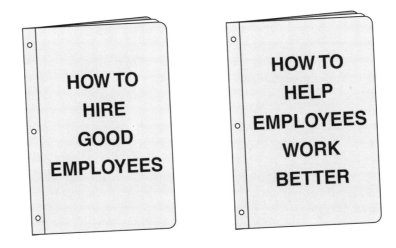

HOW TO HIRE GOOD EMPLOYEES

HOW TO HELP EMPLOYEES WORK BETTER

___*b*___ 1. Make an appointment for a meeting with the employee.

_____ 2. Ask good questions at the interview.

_____ 3. Look at the applications.

_____ 4. Tell the employee, "You can't be late every day."

_____ 5. Call past employers. Ask, "Was this person a good worker?"

_____ 6. Tell the employee, "This is how you can be on time."

Exercise C Write a memo for a class meeting. Fill in a date, time, and place. Circle things to discuss at the meeting.

M E M O

To: Students
From: ESL Teachers
Date: _____
Subject: Meeting

We will meet today at _____ (time). The meeting is _____ (place).

This is the agenda:

- school rules
- new boss
- vacation
- class schedule
- job openings
- study times
- neighborhood cleanup
- new classes

- neighborhood park
- tests and grades
- cats and dogs on street
- pay
- class party
- street lights
- parking
- other

Exercise D Think of a meeting you want to have with people at home, work, school, or another place. Write a memo for the meeting.

M E M O

To: _____
From: _____
Date: _____
Subject: Meeting

We will meet today at _____ (time). The meeting is _____ (place).

This is the agenda:

1. _____

2. _____

3. _____

Tell a partner about the meeting. Use your memo and agenda to help you.

1. Perry says, "So I am successful too." What do you think?
   Circle the words.

   Perry is successful because

he helps others.	he learned many things.
he works for a big company.	he doesn't eat lunch.
he is worried.	his work is good.

2. How do you help people at home, at your job, or at school?

   _____

   _____

3. Who helps you at home, at your job, or at school?

   _____

   _____

4. Write a question for Perry.

   _____

   _____

Chapter 4

Lee Mei Bik

Where does Mei Bik work?
What is in her office?

1   I know my life is good.
    I think, "Is my story good?"

2   My family is from **China.**
    We move to **Hong Kong.**
    My **father** is a teacher.
    He says good schools are too
    expensive in Hong Kong.
    He says, "We can find
    good schools in America."

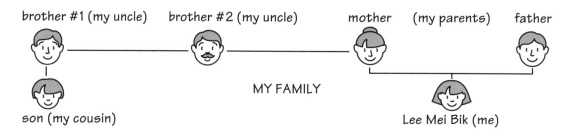

MY FAMILY

3   My **mother** has **brothers** in America.
    Brother number two is
    in Muncie, Indiana.
    He has a restaurant.
    My father can work there.
    We go to Muncie,
    but my **uncle** and my father argue.

4   Brother number one's **son**
    is in Indianapolis, Indiana.
    My father and mother say,
    "We can find jobs there."

5   We stay six months.
    My father says, "California
    has more jobs.
    It has good schools too."
    We go to San Francisco.

6   I know some English.
    I know **orange.**
    I know **apple.**
    But I can't say sentences.

7   I take ESL classes.
The **students** are
ninety-nine percent Chinese.
Some are immigrants.
Some are born in America.
They don't eat lunch at the same table.
But I like all the students.

8   I talk to my mother about life and work.
I ask, "What will I do?"
She says only, "Be happy."

9   I think. At five years old
I knew how to **multiply.**
Maybe I can be a **bookkeeper.**

10 I study bookkeeping in school.
I get **good grades.** I graduate.
I find a bookkeeping job.

11 I work with a very nice man.
He tells me, "You are smart. You
can be a certified public accountant.
You can do **tax returns.**"

U.S. Individual Tax Return Form 1040
1. Write your name.
Name: _____
Last   First
2. Write the number of people in your family on line 2.   2. _____

12 After work I go to night school.
I get a C.P.A. **license.**
My friend says, "Good for you!"
I am happy.

State License
Certified Public Accountant
Lee Mei Bik

13 One day my friend quits.
I don't ask him why,
but I think something is wrong at work.
I quit too.

14 I have a boyfriend.
One day he says,
"You aren't my girlfriend now."
My **heart breaks.**
I am very sad.

15 I go home. I look in the **mirror.**
    I say, "I am strong. I am OK.
    I can have a good life."

16 I put on nice clothes.
    I go to a nice club.
    It is the first time I go out alone.
    I meet Raymond from Kentucky.
    He is on vacation.

17 I show Raymond the **city.**
    We walk everywhere.
    People **smile** at us.
    I think, "Maybe I'm in love."

18 We get married.
    I get a wonderful new job.
    I want to keep it.
    Raymond says, "I can move to San Francisco."

19 Then Raymond gets a job
in Atlanta, Georgia.
I love my job in San Francisco.
But Raymond came to me.
Now I go with Raymond.

20 In Atlanta I find a good job.
Then Raymond's boss says,
"We have work for you in San Francisco."
We go back to San Francisco!

21 I call my boss at my old job.
I ask, "Can you give me a reference?"
He says, "Work for me."
He gives me a big **raise.**

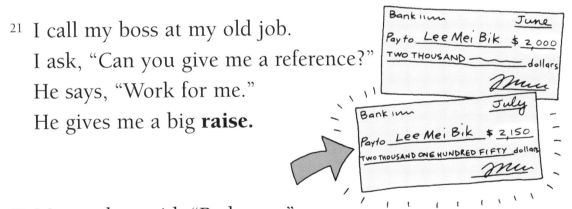

22 My mother said, "Be happy."
I love what I do.
I love where I am.
I am happy.
That is my success.

Circle *True* or *False*.

1. Mei Bik's family came to America for good schools.   (True)   False

2. Mei Bik has two uncles in San Francisco.   True   False

3. Mei Bik studied Chinese in high school.   True   False

4. She found a bookkeeping job.   True   False

5. Later she went to night school for a C.P.A. license.   True   False

6. Mei Bik moved to Georgia to find a good job.   True   False

7. Mei Bik moved back to San Francisco. Her old boss didn't help her find a job.   True   False

8. Mei Bik is not happy.   True   False

Exercise B **Match the parts of the sentences.**

___c___ 1. Mei Bik's family came to the United States because

_____ 2. Mei Bik went to night school because

_____ 3. Raymond and Mei Bik moved to Georgia because

a. she wanted to get a C.P.A. license.

b. Raymond got a job in Atlanta.

c. there are good schools in America.

Write your own answers.

4. Why do you go to school?

I go to school because I want to _____

_____.

5. Why did you move here?

I moved here because _____

_____.

Exercise C Look at the map. Find the places where Mei Bik lived. Write the missing cities and states below.

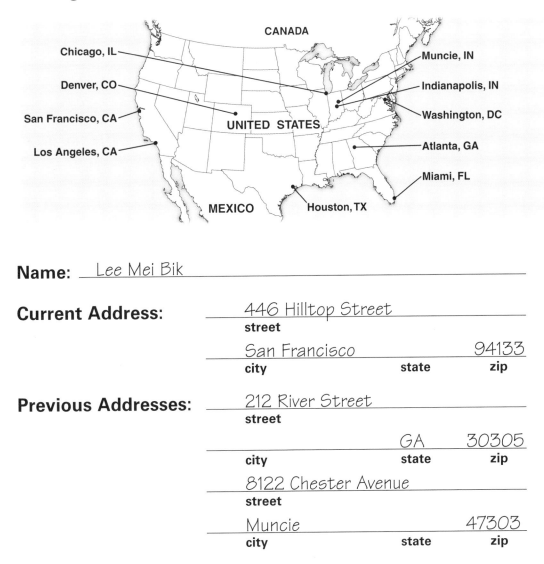

Name: Lee Mei Bik

Current Address: 446 Hilltop Street
street

San Francisco   94133
city   state   zip

Previous Addresses: 212 River Street
street

                              GA   30305
city   state   zip

8122 Chester Avenue
street

Muncie   47303
city   state   zip

Exercise D Fill in your name, current address, and a previous address in the United States. Write the city or cities on the map above.

Name: _____

Current Address: _____
street

_____
city   state   zip

Previous Address: _____
street

_____
city   state   zip

Exercise E Match the contractions with the full forms of the words.

Contractions	Full Forms
_d_ 1. can't	a. are not
___ 2. it's	b. do not
___ 3. aren't	c. he is
___ 4. I'm	d. can not
___ 5. don't	e. it is
___ 6. he's	f. I am
___ 7. I'll	g. I will

Exercise F Write the business/job words and the school words. Some words can be both.

study	boss	classes	multiply	reference
	good grades		raise	tax returns

Business/Job

boss

_____

_____

_____

School

_____

_____

_____

Exercise G Say these words. Listen for the sound of *oo*. Circle the letters that make the *oo* sound in the words.

1. sch(oo)l   4. new

2. you   5. move

3. to   6. argue

Mei Bik's Day at the Office

1 I go to work at 9:00 or 10:00 A.M.
It is my decision.

2 I read accounting magazines.
I study new laws.

3 My first client arrives at 11:00.
Her company sells cookies.
I give her the tax form.
She gives me cookies.

4 At noon my boss gives
me a big **file.**
He says, "Please do this
tax return."
I say, "I'll be happy to do it."

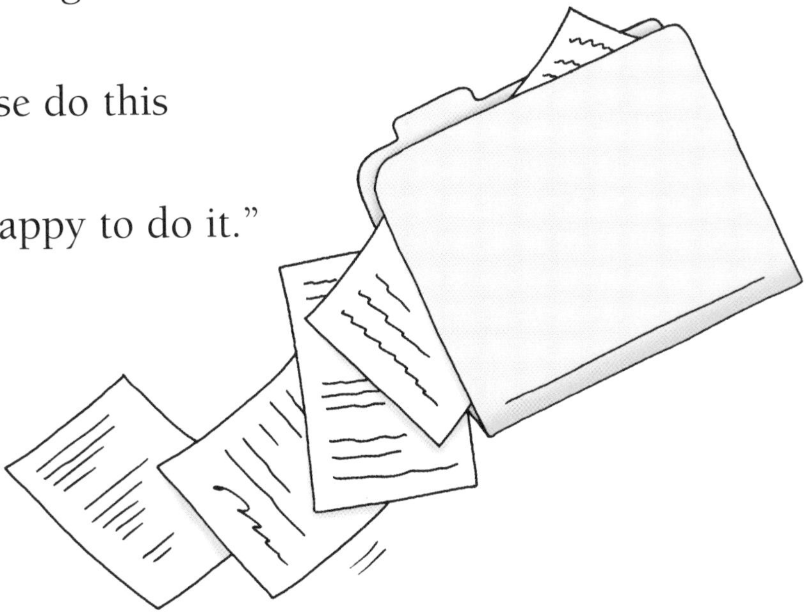

5 At 1:00 P.M. I see my second client.
   He has property and money.
   I look at his papers.
   Tax returns tell stories about people.
   It's like reading a book.

6 I eat a **sandwich** at 2:00.
   I do more tax returns.
   At 7:15 I finish my work.
   Then I help my **co-workers** finish.

7 I look at my **calendar.**
   Tomorrow morning I come in at 9:00.

8 By 8:00 in the evening I am home.
   I am with Raymond.
   I feel my life is very, very good.

Exercise A Mei Bik is looking for the files of some of her clients. The files are in the order of the alphabet.* Look at the letters and numbers on the drawers of the file cabinet. Circle the number of the drawer for each file.

A-F ①	G-L ②	M-P ③
Q-T ④	U-Z ⑤	🔑

1. Garcia,   Isabel   1   ②   3   4   5
   Last Name,   **First Name**

2. Tucker,   David   1   2   3   4   5
   Last Name,   **First Name**

3. Norton,   Miro   1   2   3   4   5
   Last Name,   **First Name**

4. Beda,   Patricia   1   2   3   4   5
   Last Name,   **First Name**

5. Singh,   Amarjit   1   2   3   4   5
   Last Name,   **First Name**

6. Carnes,   Marie   1   2   3   4   5
   Last Name,   **First Name**

7. Young,   Natasha   1   2   3   4   5
   Last Name,   **First Name**

8. Perez,   Ines   1   2   3   4   5
   Last Name,   **First Name**

Ask a partner about the files.

Examples: *Where is the file for Isabel Garcia?*
What is David's last name?

*The Alphabet:

A B C D E F G H I J K L M N O P Q R S T U V W X Y Z

Exercise B Write your name on line 1. Write the names of some friends on the other lines. Then circle the number of the drawer for each one.

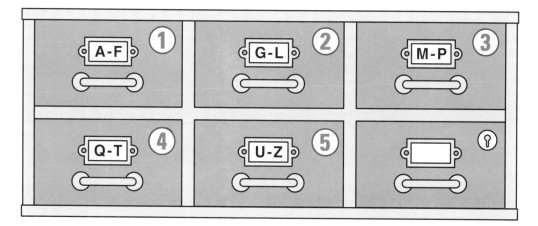

1. _____   1   2   3   4   5
    Last Name,   **First Name**

2. _____   1   2   3   4   5
    Last Name,   **First Name**

3. _____   1   2   3   4   5
    Last Name,   **First Name**

4. _____   1   2   3   4   5
    Last Name,   **First Name**

5. _____   1   2   3   4   5
    Last Name,   **First Name**

6. _____   1   2   3   4   5
    Last Name,   **First Name**

7. _____   1   2   3   4   5
    Last Name,   **First Name**

8. _____   1   2   3   4   5
    Last Name,   **First Name**

Tell a partner about the files.

Examples: *My file is in drawer 4.*

           Ana's file is in drawer 2.

Step One:

Get the U.S. Government **tax booklet.**
Get the U.S. Individual Income
Tax Return form too.

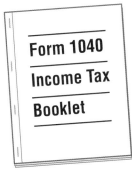

Form 1040
Income Tax
Booklet

Step Two:

Get the **W-2 Wage and
Tax Statement**
from your employer.
Get an **interest statement**
from your bank.
The **amounts** of money on these
forms are earnings.

State	Employer's state I.D. no.	State wages, tips, etc.	State income tax	Local income tax
CA	578-00341	14,987.02	461.76	0.00

W-2 Wage and Tax Statement
Copy for Employee's Records

INTEREST   STATEMENT

Savings account #123456-00   Lena Collins

Total interest paid: $ 92.25

$14,987.02
$92.25

Step Three:

Get records of **doctor bills.**
Get records of business expenses
like telephone bills.
The amounts of money on these
bills are deductions.

OFFICES OF
Harold Cochrane, MD

Office visit 9/24 $ 35.00

Step Four:

Write the amounts on the tax form.

Step Five:

Sign and **mail** the tax form!

Look at "How to Prepare a Tax Return." Write the correct words
from the box under the pictures.

> mail   tax booklet   wage and tax statement   sign
> interest statement   amounts

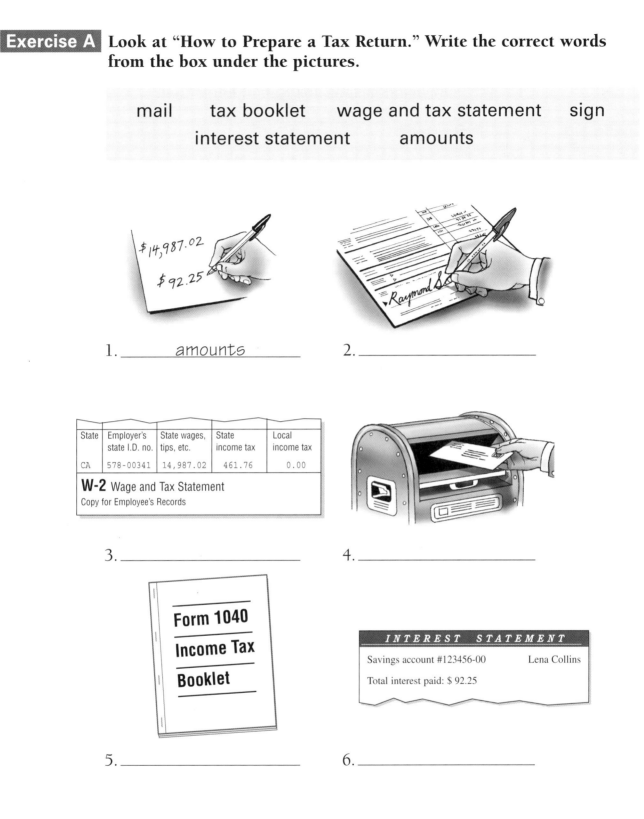

1. _____ amounts _____   2. _____

State	Employer's state I.D. no.	State wages, tips, etc.	State income tax	Local income tax
CA	578-00341	14,987.02	461.76	0.00

W-2 Wage and Tax Statement
Copy for Employee's Records

3. _____   4. _____

Form 1040
Income Tax
Booklet

INTEREST STATEMENT

Savings account #123456-00   Lena Collins

Total interest paid: $ 92.25

5. _____   6. _____

Follow the directions. Use the chart below to help you.

U.S. Individual Income Tax Return Form 1040		
1. Write your name. Name: _____ Last _____ First		
2. Write the number of people in your family on line 2.	2.	_____
3. Multiply line 2 by $1,500.00. Write the answer on line 3.		
	3.	_____ . _____
4. Add the earnings: $14,500.00, $8,500.00, $92.25. Write the total earnings on line 4.		
	4.	_____ . _____
5. Add the deductions: $375.00, $422.00. Write the total deductions on line 5.		
	5.	_____ . _____
6. Subtract line 5 from line 4. Write the answer on line 6.		
	6.	_____ . _____
7. Subtract line 3 from line 6. Write the answer on line 7.		
	7.	_____ . _____
8. Sign your name on line 8.	8.	_____

Direction Word	Symbol	Example
Add	+	25 + 10 = 35
Subtract	−	100 - 80 = 20
Multiply	x	8 x 10 = 80
Sign		*Lee Mei Bik*

Ask a partner about the numbers.

Examples: *What amount is on line 7?*

What number is on line 2?

Look at the W-2 Wage and Tax Statement. Find the information. Write the words.

a Control number b Employer identification number 03-073551	1 Wages, tips, other earnings 14,987.02	2 Federal income tax withheld 1,846.74
c Employer's name, address, and ZIP code Mrs. B's Best Cookies P.O. Box 318 San Fresca, CA 91000	3 Social security wages 15,223.60 5 Medicare wages and tips 15,223.60	4 Social security tax withheld 971.52 6 Medicare tax withheld 227.28
d Employee's social security number 072-15-8892 e Employee's name, address, and ZIP Code Lena Collins 218 North Lake Dr. Valleha, CA 90123	7 Advance ECI payment 9 Benefits included in box 1	8 Dependent care benefits 10 Other 153.92

State CA	Employer's state I.D. no. 578-00341	State wages, tips, etc. 14,987.02	State income tax 461.76	Local income tax 0.00

W-2 Wage and Tax Statement
Copy for Employee's Records

1. Employee's name   _Lena Collins_____

2. Earnings $_____

3. Federal income tax   _____

4. State income tax   _____

5. Local income tax   _____

1. Mei Bik says, "I know my life is good." Why do you think she says that?

   Circle the sentences.

   She is not good at math.   She likes her work.

   She knows English.   She lives in San Francisco.

   She helps clients.   She is not strong.

   She doesn't help her co-workers.

2. Mei Bik is good at bookkeeping and accounting. What are you good at?

   _____

   _____

3. What makes you happy?

   _____

   _____

4. Write a question for Mei Bik.

   _____

   _____

Chapter 5

Sergio Gonzalez

Where does Sergio work?
What does he do?

1 People in the United States
go to Mexicali to buy things.
They buy hats, pictures, and **sarapes.**

2 Mexicali is a town on the **border**
between the United States and Mexico.
I was born there.
Everybody knew me in Mexicali.
I learned to behave there.
I learned **respect** there.

3 My father, mother, brother, and I
came to the United States on vacation.
Then my father found a job.
So he and my mother decided to stay.
My little brother stayed too.

4 My **parents** sent me back to Mexico.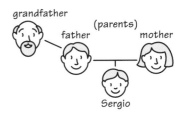
They wanted me to finish my
school year.
I lived with my **grandfather** and
my uncle.
I missed my family a lot.
When I was bad,
they **yelled** at me.
I missed that.

5 After a year my father came for me.
Our family moved into a big room
in my uncle's **backyard.**

6 I started high school in the tenth grade.
I didn't know anybody.
Then I saw a friend from Mexicali!
He helped me find my classes.

7   In math class
a teacher asked me a question in English.
I didn't understand the words.
I was embarrassed.
Students laughed at me.
I tried not to think about it.

8   On the **bus** I saw a guy eating
and **drinking.**
He said, "What are you looking at
I got off the bus.

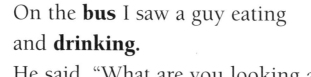

9   In P.E. I had a friend in a gang.
He said, "Get into it.
You'll have fun, meet girls,
and go to **parties.**"
But I didn't.
I knew I could get hurt.

10 I was starting my new life.
    I practiced speaking English.
    I read, studied, and did my homework.

11 The first thing I learned was,
    "What is your favorite day of the week?"
    I knew the answer: **Saturday.**

12 Then suddenly my parents **separated.**
    There was nothing I could do.
    I felt sad.
    My mother and brother moved.
    I stayed with my dad.

13 We needed money.
    I got a job cooking **hamburgers.**
    I worked 40 hours a week,
    sometimes more.

Sergio Gonzalez	Report Card			
English	F			
Art	F			
Math	F			
P.E.	F			

¹⁴ I started to **fail** all my classes.
My teachers asked,
"Oh, what's happening, Sergio?"
I didn't answer.
I didn't want to tell them my problems.

¹⁵ I needed to work full-time.
I also wanted to go to school
and get good grades.

¹⁶ I got a new job with more pay,
benefits, and a vacation.
The job is **painting** buildings,
and I like it.

¹⁷ I'm getting good grades again,
and I like that.

18 I can say, "A lot of bad things happened:
I left my country and my friends.
My parents separated.
I needed to go to school and work full-time.
But in life there are always problems.
I face them and look what happens!

19 I graduate.
I get my high school diploma!"

Exercise A **Circle *True* or *False*.**

1. Sergio's family came to the United States
   for a vacation. (True) False

2. Sergio and his brother went back to Mexico. True False

3. Sergio missed his family. True False

4. In school Sergio didn't understand all the
   English words. True False

5. He wanted to get into a gang. True False

6. Sergio worked 40 hours a week. True False

7. Now Sergio has a good job with benefits
   and a vacation. True False

8. Sergio didn't finish high school. True False

Exercise B **Complete the sentences.**

1. Sergio's family stayed in the United States because

   his father found a job .

2. Sergio was embarrassed at school because

   _____ .

3. Sometimes I feel embarrassed because

   _____ .

4. Sergio changed jobs because his family needed

   _____ .

5. I (will / will not) change jobs because

   _____

   _____ .

Exercise C Look at the story again. Imagine you are Sergio. Fill in the form about Sergio and his job.

Name: _Sergio Gonzalez_

Application for _____
(job)

Check (✓) the times you can work.

_____ full-time (40 hrs./week)

_____ part-time (20 hrs./week)

_____ days

_____ nights

_____ weekends (Saturday/Sunday)

Do you have a high school diploma or G.E.D.?

_____ yes   _____ no

 Exercise D Fill in the form with your name and your own answers.

Name: _____

Application for _____
(job)

Check (✓) the times you can work.

_____ full-time (40 hrs./week)

_____ part-time (20 hrs./week)

_____ days

_____ nights

_____ weekends (Saturday/Sunday)

Do you have a high school diploma or G.E.D.?

_____ yes   _____ no

Look at the words in the box. Complete the sentences with the plurals.

one *(singular)*	two or more *(plural)*
hat party class	hat + s = hats party + s = parties class + s = classes

1. Sergio passed all his high school (class) _____classes_____.

2. He has friends in two (city) _____.

3. Sergio takes (bus) _____ to school.

4. Sergio works about 40 (hour) _____ a week.

5. Sergio talked to his (friend) _____.

Exercise F Write the words about problems and the words about good things. Some words can be both.

separated	fun	benefits	fail	respect
	embarrassed	vacation	gang	

Problems   **Good Things**

_____separated_____   _____

_____   _____

_____   _____

_____   _____

Exercise G Listen to the sound of *th* in *this* and *father*. Find other words from the story with the same sound. Write them on the lines.

_____mother_____   _____   _____

_____   _____   _____

1   I get up at 5:00 in the morning.
     I take a **shower.**
     At 6:00 I go to work.

2   I **drive** about 45 minutes.
     It depends on **traffic.**
     I buy coffee every day.
     I drink it.
     Then I start work.
     I paint buildings.

3   At 12:00 I finish work.
     I drive home.
     I take another shower
     and dress for school.
     I eat lunch and go to class.

4 After school I go home.
   I do my homework
   for one or two hours.
   I **wash** my painting clothes.
   I clean my house.

5 For dinner I get **tacos** or
   eat **Chinese food.**

6 Before I go to bed,
   I call my girlfriend, or she calls me.
   She asks me what happened at work.
   Then I go to sleep.

Exercise A Look at the chart about Sergio's day. Write the times he arrives.

Sergio leaves at	He drives	He arrives at
(home) 6:00 A.M.	45 minutes	6:45 A.M.
6:15 A.M.	45 minutes	_____
6:30 A.M.	45 minutes	_____
(work) 12:00 P.M.	45 minutes	_____
12:45 P.M.	45 minutes	_____
1:30 P.M.	45 minutes	_____

Ask a partner about Sergio's day.

Example: Student A: *Sergio leaves home at 6:00.*
What time does he arrive at work?
Student B: *He arrives at 6:45.*

Exercise B Complete the chart about your day. What time do you leave home, work, or school? How much time do you drive, ride, or walk? What time do you arrive?

I leave at	I drive/ride/walk	I arrive at
(home) _____	_____	_____
(work/ school) _____	_____	_____

Ask a partner about his or her chart.

Examples: *What time do you leave home?*
How long do you drive, ride, or walk?
What time do you arrive?

1   Put on white painter's pants,
    a shirt, work boots,
    and a **hard hat.**

2   Choose water-base paint
    for outside.

3   Take your paint and **tools.**
    Get on the **scaffold.**
    Push the button
    and go up.

4   Get your **roller.**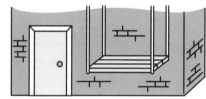
    Put paint on it.
    Now paint the **walls** up and down.

5   Finish painting.
    Push the button and go down.
    Wash the roller.
    Wash the **bucket.**
    Say good-bye to your co-workers.

Exercise A Look again at "How to Paint a Building." Write the correct words from the box on the lines.

scaffold   bucket   paint   hard hat   roller   wall

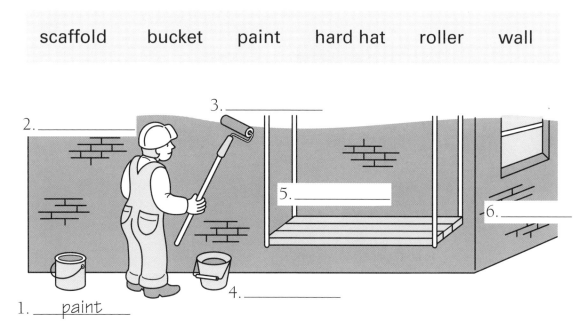

2. _____

3. _____

5. _____

6. _____

4. _____

1. ___paint___

Exercise B Sergio is teaching a new co-worker how to paint a building. Number the sentences in the correct order.

_____ Before you paint, put paint on the roller.

_____ Paint the walls up and down.

_____ Push the button and go up.

___1___ Before you work, put on a hard hat.

_____ Before you leave, wash the tools and say good-bye.

_____ After you finish painting, push the button and go down.

_____ Then take your paint and get on the scaffold.

Ask a partner about the directions.

Examples: *What do you do before you paint?*
What do you do after you finish painting?

Exercise C Look for these words and symbols on the labels below.

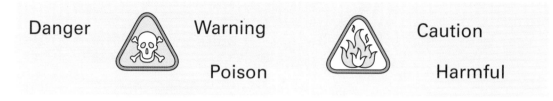

Danger   Warning   Caution

Poison   Harmful

Now look at the labels again. Circle the words and symbols that mean *dangerous*.

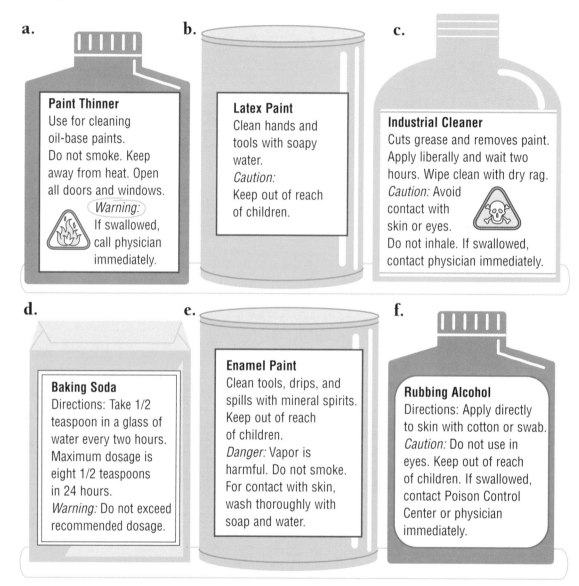

a.

Paint Thinner
Use for cleaning
oil-base paints.
Do not smoke. Keep
away from heat. Open
all doors and windows.
Warning:
If swallowed,
call physician
immediately.

b.

Latex Paint
Clean hands and
tools with soapy
water.
Caution:
Keep out of reach
of children.

c.

Industrial Cleaner
Cuts grease and removes paint.
Apply liberally and wait two
hours. Wipe clean with dry rag.
Caution: Avoid
contact with
skin or eyes.
Do not inhale. If swallowed,
contact physician immediately.

d.

Baking Soda
Directions: Take 1/2
teaspoon in a glass of
water every two hours.
Maximum dosage is
eight 1/2 teaspoons
in 24 hours.
Warning: Do not exceed
recommended dosage.

e.

Enamel Paint
Clean tools, drips, and
spills with mineral spirits.
Keep out of reach
of children.
Danger: Vapor is
harmful. Do not smoke.
For contact with skin,
wash thoroughly with
soap and water.

f.

Rubbing Alcohol
Directions: Apply directly
to skin with cotton or swab.
Caution: Do not use in
eyes. Keep out of reach
of children. If swallowed,
contact Poison Control
Center or physician
immediately.

Talk about the labels with a partner.

Example: Student A: *Be careful with that enamel paint.*
Student B: *Why?*
Student A: *It says, "Danger: Vapor is harmful."*

Exercise D Look at labels on things you have at home or at work. Write the names of four items. Check (✓) the warning words and symbols you see on the labels.

Warning Words and Symbols					
	Danger	**Poison**	**Warning**	**Caution**	
paint thinner	✓	✓			

 Exercise E Look at the painters. Write three things they are doing wrong.

1.   <u>One man is not wearing a hard hat.</u>

2.   _____

3.   _____

4.   _____

Tell a partner about the problems.

1. What do you think about Sergio?

   Circle the words.

   a. Sergio is successful because he has

a good job.	friends.	a high school diploma.
a vacation.	benefits.	a full-time job.

   b. Sergio is successful because he

faces problems.	misses his family.	is in a gang.
gets good grades.	works hard.	studied hard.

   didn't tell his teachers about his problems.

2. Sergio buys a cup of coffee every day. What is something you do every day?

   _____

   _____

3. Write a question for Sergio.

   _____

   _____

Chapter 6

Yenework Alemayehu

Date: Sept 7

Where does Yenework work?
What does she do?

Yenework, Teacher and Social Worker

1 I was born in **Ethiopia.**
   I lived in the capital city.
   My father worked for the **king** of
   my country.
   The king was our friend.

2 When I was in high school
   I said, "I want to go to college."
   But in Ethiopia there was only one college.
   In America there are lots of colleges.

3 My cousin was in school in Ohio.
   He said, "You can come to Ohio.
   You can live with an American family."
   I wanted to do that.
   My parents said, "Go!"

4 My American family lived in
   Wayne, Ohio.
   There was one **street.**
   There was a **post office,**
   a **grocery store,**
   and a little **diner.**
   I said, "Huh? Where is the city?"

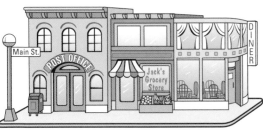

5 My high school was in a **cornfield.**
   I saw boys and girls **hold hands**
   at school.
   I thought, "Huh?
   American culture is different!"

6 I was the first foreign student in the school.
   The students wanted to know about me.

7 They asked, "Do you ride **elephants**
to school?"
They asked, "Don't you have a nickname?"
I said, "Listen. I can say *George*. You
can say *Yenework*."
I said, "You say *twenny*.
But the word is *twenty*."
I said, "You Americans talk through
your **noses.**"
I had fun in high school.

8 I got a scholarship to Bluffton College.
Bluffton is a Mennonite college.
I said, "That isn't my religion."
They said, "It's OK. Come."
I studied hard in college.
I didn't have time to make friends.

9 Then there was a revolution in my country.
My family was in danger.
I wanted to go home.
My family said, "Stay!"

10 But my family couldn't send
   any more money.
   My scholarship didn't pay all the **tuition.**
   I owed money.
   I couldn't graduate.

COLLEGE

Spring Semester
Tuition $5,000.00

Amount Due   *$5,000.00*

11 The college president was very nice.
   He said, "Yenework, study for your exams.
   You will have what you need."

12 For three days I studied.
   Then I got a **telephone call.**
   The president's assistant said,
   "Come to our office."

13 A man and a woman were there.
   The president said, "Yenework,
   this is Mr. and Mrs. Winkler.
   They want to help a good student.
   They want to pay your tuition."
   I couldn't believe it.
   I said, "Huh?"

14 The Winklers came to my graduation.
   They said, "What will you do now?"
   I said, "I don't know. I'm on a student visa.
   But I don't have money for graduate school."
   They said, "We can pay for graduate school."
   I said, "Huh?"

15 So I got a master's degree in education.
   I found a government job.
   I did social work.
   I helped families with problems.
   I bought furniture for my **apartment.**

16 Then the government ran out of money.
   I was laid off.
   I could not pay my rent!

17 A friend said, "You can teach in an adult school."
I taught three hours at night.
I drove 45 minutes each way.
I loved to teach!
Then the **government agency** called me.
They had money to pay social workers again.
I went back to my full-time job.

18 Now I teach ESL at night,
and in the daytime I help families.
My students know about worry and **fear.**
My families know about worry and fear.
I know about worry and fear too.
I tell people, "Do your best work.
Good comes."

Circle *True* or *False*.

1. Yenework came to the United States to go
   to graduate school.   True   (False)

2. At first she lived in a big city in Ohio.   True   False

3. American culture is different from
   Ethiopian culture.   True   False

4. Yenework needed more money to pay the
   college tuition.   True   False

5. Mr. and Mrs. Winkler helped Yenework
   find a job.   True   False

6. A social worker helps families.   True   False

7. Yenework teaches ESL at night.   True   False

8. Yenework understands families and students.   True   False

Exercise B **Answer the questions.**

1. Who helped Yenework pay for college and graduate school?

   _____ Mr. and Mrs. Winkler _____ helped pay for college

   and graduate school.

2. In the daytime, who does Yenework help now?

   In the daytime she helps _____.

3. Who else does Yenework help?

   _____.

4. Who helped you at school or at work?

   _____ helped me.

5. Who do you help?

   I help _____.

Who helped Yenework? Complete the sentences with the correct words from the box.

friend   college   president   cousin   a man and a woman

Problems

1. Yenework wanted to go to college in the United States.

2. Yenework needed money to go to college.

3. Her family could not send more money.

4. Yenework didn't have money for graduate school.

5. Yenework was laid off.

Who helped Yenework?

Her _____cousin_____ in Ohio told her to come.

A Mennonite _____ gave her a scholarship.

The college _____ told her to study for the exams.

_____ paid for graduate school.

Her _____ told her about a job.

Exercise D Interview a partner. Ask: "What problems do people have?" Ask: "Who can help?" Write the problems. Write some people or places that can help.

Problems	Who can help?
1.	
2.	
3.	

Read the sentences. Choose the correct words from the box to complete the sentences.

night	laid off	city	problems	different

1. Wayne, Ohio, is a small town. It's not a big _____city_____ .

2. Yenework is a social worker. She helps families

   with _____ .

3. The government agency ran out of money. Yenework

   was _____ .

4. Yenework doesn't teach in the morning. She teaches

   at _____ .

5. American culture and Ethiopian culture are not the same.

   They are _____ .

Look at the letter groups in the box. Fill in the blanks with the correct letter groups to make words from the story. You can use some letter groups more than once.

gr-	str-	pr-	thr-	fr-

1. In Wayne, Ohio, there was only one _str_ eet.

2. There was a _____ ocery store.

3. Yenework's _____ iend helped her find a job.

4. She couldn't _____ aduate because she owed money.

5. The college _____ esident was very nice.

6. Yenework studied for _____ ee days.

7. She got a master's de _____ ee in education.

8. Now she helps families with ____ oblems.

1   From 7:30 A.M. until 5:00 P.M.
I am a social worker.
I work with children who have problems.
I work with their families too.
They don't want problems,
but sometimes they don't want
a social worker!

2   I understand the families.
I try to help them.
I teach parenting skills.
I talk about **health care.**
I help families stay together.
I also find agencies that can help them.
My job is important,
but it is not always fun.

3   From 6:30 P.M. until 9:00 P.M.
    I am a teacher.
    I teach ESL to adults.
    This job is important too.
    My students like the class.
    They want to learn.
    For me this job is always fun.

4   I leave the house at 7:00 A.M.
    I get home at 9:30 P.M.
    For breakfast I drink a cup of **tea.**
    Lunch is at 12:00 or when I have time.
    After I leave my day job I go to
    my night job.
    On the way I eat **fast food** for dinner.

5   I think I am too busy!

Look at the government services information below. Write the agency telephone numbers next to the problems.

GOVERNMENT SERVICES INFORMATION			
Bradford Adult Education	226-7550	Food & Fuel Assistance	225-3333
Children's Aid Society	371-9922	Northland City Hospital	371-4000
Employment & Training	225-1616	Senior Citizen Center	922-9110
Emergency (Fire/Police)	911		

Type of Problem   **Telephone Number**

1. health   _371-4000_

2. employment/job   _____

3. family   _____

4. children   _____

5. food   _____

6. older people/senior citizens   _____

7. fire   _____

Work with a partner. Imagine you are calling about a problem.

Example: Student A: *I need help with a job.*

Student B: *Call Employment and Training at 225-1616.*

Exercise B Look in a telephone book for government services information in your neighborhood. Write the name and telephone number of an agency for each of the problems.

GOVERNMENT SERVICES INFORMATION

Agency Name | Telephone Number

_____ | _____

(health care)

_____ | _____

(emergency)

_____ | _____

(family)

_____ | _____

(children)

_____ | _____

(employment)

_____ | _____

(women)

_____ | _____

(older people/senior citizens)

1   You and your child are
in a grocery store.
Your child wants **candy.**
You say, "No."

2   Your child gets angry.
Maybe your child **jumps**
up and down and yells.
Children don't understand "No."
They think it means, "I don't love you."
Say to your child, "I love you.
We need a time out."
Go outside and **walk.**

3   Is your child **quiet**?
Say, "We can **go inside** now.
We won't buy candy, but you
can choose the best apple
in the box."

Exercise A Look at "A Parenting Skill." Write the correct words from the box under the pictures.

walk   go inside   quiet   candy   jumps

1. _____go inside_____

2. _____

3. _____

4. _____

5. _____

Exercise B Think about what the parent and child say in the grocery store. Number the lines in order.

_____   Parent: "We can go inside now."

_____   Parent: "I love you."

___1___   Child: "I want candy."

_____   Parent: "No."

_____   Parent: "We won't buy candy, but you can choose the

best apple."

_____   Parent: "We need a time out."

_____   Child: "I *want* candy!"

Work with a partner. Act out the conversation.

Exercise C Look at the pictures. Imagine you are the store employee. What can you say to the customer or what can you do? Write a sentence for each picture.

_____

_____

It's broken! It doesn't work!

_____

_____

_____

_____

Exercise D Think of a time at home, school, or work. Someone gets angry. What do you say or do? Draw a picture and write about it.

_____

_____

1. Yenework says, "Do your best work." What did Yenework do to be successful?

   _____

   _____

2. She says, "Good comes." What good things do you think came to Yenework?

   _____

   _____

3. People helped Yenework. Now she helps others. Why is it important for people to help one another?

   _____

   _____

4. Write a question for Yenework.

   _____

   _____

Answer Key

Chapter 1

Part 1

Exercise A, p. 7

2. False
3. True
4. True
5. True
6. False
7. True
8. False

Exercise B, p. 7

2. bakery
3. Answers will vary.
4. Answers will vary.

Exercise C, p. 8

Answers will vary.

Exercise D, p. 8

Answers will vary.

Exercise E, p. 9

2. baker
3. baked
4. bakes

Exercise F, p. 9

Food: bread, vegetables, butter, cream
Feelings: angry, lazy, happy, lucky

Exercise G, p. 9

2. butter
3. cut
4. luck
5. customer

Part 2

Exercise A, p. 12

3:30 goes to the bakery
2:00 sleeps
8:00 or 9:00 goes home

Exercise B, p. 13

Answers will vary.

Part 3

Exercise A, p. 16

4   1
6   3
5   2

Exercise B, p. 17

2. add
3. chop
4. preheat
5. mix
6. drop

Exercise C, p. 18

1 lb brown sugar
10 oz peanut butter
3 1/2 c flour
1/4 tsp baking powder
1/4 tsp baking soda
1/2 tsp salt
1 c peanuts

Exercise D, p. 19

2 lb brown sugar
20 oz peanut butter (or 1 lb 4 oz)
7 c flour
1/2 tsp baking powder
1/2 tsp baking soda
1 tsp salt
2 c peanuts

Exercise E, p. 19

Answers will vary.

Chapter 2

Part 1

Exercise A, p. 28

2. False
3. False
4. True
5. True
6. True
7. True
8. False

Exercise B, p. 28

2. Los Angeles
3. Answers will vary.
4. Answers will vary.

Exercise C, p. 29

12
10

Exercise D, p. 29

2. 80
3. 38
4. 10
5. 20

Exercise E, p. 30

2. going
3. knitting
4. selling

Exercise F, p. 30

Clothing Business: sweaters, hand loom, knit, store
Family: husband, marry, children, daughter

Exercise G, p. 30

2.
3.
4.
5.
6. ✓
7. ✓
8. ✓

Part 2

Exercise A, p. 33

2. f
3. e
4. a
5. b
6. d

Exercise B, p. 34

Answers will vary.

Part 3

Exercise A, p. 37

2. return address
3. (padded) envelope
4. color
5. style number
6. size

Exercise B, p. 38

2. d
3. b
4. a

Exercise C, p. 39

Answers will vary.

Exercise D, p. 39

Answers will vary.

Chapter 3

Part 1

Exercise A, p. 48

2. True
3. False
4. True
5. False
6. False
7. False
8. True

Exercise B, p. 48

Answers will vary.

Exercise C, p. 49

a. busboy
b. lawyer
c. inventory control manager

Exercise D, p. 49

2. a, c
3. a, c
4. c
5. b, c

Exercise E, p. 49

Answers will vary.

Exercise F, p. 50

2. law school
3. law
4. laws

Exercise G, p. 50

School: study, learn, professor, graduate
Job: company, interview, employers, employees, (learn, professor)

Exercise H, p. 50

2. a
3. o
4. aw
5. a

Part 2

Exercise A, p. 53

2. c
3. a
4. a
5. b

Exercise B, p. 54

Answers will vary.

Part 3

Exercise A, p. 55

2. c
3. b
4. a
5. f
6. d

Exercise B, p. 56

2. a
3. a
4. b
5. a
6. b

Exercise C, p. 57

Answers will vary.

Exercise D, p. 57

Answers will vary.

Chapter 4

Part 1

Exercise A, p. 66

2. False
3. False
4. True
5. True
6. False
7. False
8. False

Exercise B, p. 66

2. a
3. b
4. Answers will vary.
5. Answers will vary.

Exercise C, p. 67

CA; Atlanta; IN

Exercise D, p. 67

Answers will vary.

Exercise E, p. 68

2. e
3. a
4. f
5. b
6. c
7. g

Exercise F, p. 68

Business/Job: boss, reference, raise, tax returns, (multiply)
School: study, classes, multiply, good grades, (reference)

Exercise G, p. 68

2. ou
3. o
4. ew
5. o
6. ue

Part 2

Exercise A, p. 71

2. 4
3. 3
4. 1
5. 4
6. 1
7. 5
8. 3

Exercise B, p. 72

Answers will vary.

Part 3

Exercise A, p. 75

2. sign
3. wage and tax statement
4. mail
5. tax booklet
6. interest statement

Exercise B, p. 76

1. Answers will vary.
2. Answers will vary.
3. Answers will vary.
4. $23,092.25
5. $797.00
6. $22,295.25
7 Answers will vary.
8. Answers will vary.

Exercise C, p. 77

2. $14,987.02
3. $1,846.74
4. $461.76
5. 0.00

Chapter 5

Part 1

Exercise A, p. 86

2. False
3. True
4. True
5. False
6. True
7. True
8. False

Exercise B, p. 86

2. he didn't understand the words (teacher).
3. Answers will vary.
4. money
5. Answers will vary.

Exercise C, p. 87

Application for painter
(All items checked. All are possible.)
yes or no

Exercise D, p. 87

Answers will vary.

Exercise E, p. 88

2. cities
3. buses
4. hours
5. friends

Exercise F, p. 88

Problems: separated, fail, embarrassed, gang, (benefits, vacation)
Good Things: fun, benefits, respect, vacation

Exercise G, p. 88

Answers will vary, but include brother, the, then, there, grandfather, they, that, them

Part 2

Exercise A, p. 91

He arrives at...
7:00 A.M.
7:15 A.M.
12:45 P.M.
1:30 P.M.
2:15 P.M.

Exercise B, p. 91

Answers will vary.

Part 3

Exercise A, p. 93

2. hard hat
3. roller
4. bucket
5. scaffold
6. wall

Exercise B, p. 93

4
5
3
1
7
6
2

Exercise C, p. 94

a. *Warning,*
b. *Caution*
c. *Caution,*
d. *Warning*
e. *Danger, Harmful*
f. *Caution, Poison*

Exercise D, p. 95

Answers will vary.

Exercise E, p. 95

Answers will vary, but include:
2. One man is smoking near the paint can.
3. The woman is stirring her coffee with a screwdriver (or tool).
4. The woman is wearing sandals (or open-toed shoes).
5. The ladder is off the ground on one side.

Chapter 6

Part 1

Exercise A, p. 104

2. False
3. True
4. True
5. False
6. True
7. True
8. True

Exercise B, p. 104

2. families
3. students
4. Answers will vary.
5. Answers will vary.

Exercise C, p. 105

2. college
3. president
4. A man and a woman
5. friend

Exercise D, p. 105

Answers will vary.

Exercise E, p. 106

2. problems
3. laid off
4. night
5. different

Exercise F, p. 106

2. gr
3. fr
4. gr
5. pr
6. thr
7. gr
8. pr

Part 2

Exercise A, p. 109

2. 225-1616
3. 371-9922 or 225-3333
4. 371-9922
5. 225-3333
6. 922-9110
7. 911

Exercise B, p. 110

Answers will vary.

Part 3

Exercise A, p. 112

2. walk
3. jumps
4. quiet
5. candy

Exercise B, p. 112

6
4
1
2
7
5
3

Exercise C, p. 113

Answers will vary.

Exercise D, p. 113

Answers will vary.

Chapter-Specific Teaching Notes

Chapter 1— David Tran [Dā vid Trän]
Related Topics from *The Oxford Picture Dictionary:*

- Food: pages 50–59
- Work: pages 136–140
- Daily Routines: pages 26–27

Part 1

Culture Cue: Discuss the four-leaf clover as a symbol of good luck. Ask students about symbols of luck in their cultures.

Exercises C & D: Help learners talk about their own jobs/desired jobs/skills. Ask:
What is David's job? What is your job? What skills does David have? What can you do?

Compare and Contrast: Prepare a chart for learners to complete. For example:

David	(Learner's Name)
He was a _____ in his country.	I was a _____ in my country.

Write and Draw: Learners may write about and illustrate their jobs.

Exercises E-G: Follow up by asking learners to write simple sentences using the words from the exercises.

Part 2

Exercises A & B: Help students tell time on an analog clock and a digital clock. Learners might interview each other and record their partners' activities. Point out differences in simple present tense verb forms for *I* and *he/she.*

Part 3

Total Physical Response: Use TPR techniques to introduce and practice recipe instructions.

Exercise D: You may want to do this exercise together as a large group. Have learners measure and then double the amounts in the recipe. Depending on the level of the class, you may want to show that "1/2 tsp + 1/2 tsp = 1 tsp," introduce "16 oz = 1 lb," or have learners change "20 oz" to pounds and ounces.

Follow-up: Have learners find weights and measurements on food boxes. Compare metric and standard measurements.

Dictation: Dictate simple statements. Depending on the level of the class, learners can write the entire sentence or just the time or measurement amounts. For example: *I get up at 7:00. I need 2 cups of sugar.*

Song: If there are young parents in the class, you might enjoy teaching them the nursery rhyme "Patty Cake."

Additional Discussion: Ask questions such as: *Do you like to bake? Why or why not?*

Wrap-up: Encourage learners to think of questions they would like to ask David. As a group, guess what David's answer might be.

Chapter 2 — Suss Carlsson Cousins [Sōōs Carl son Cou sins]
Related Topics from *The Oxford Picture Dictionary:*

- Clothing: pages 64–65, 70–71
- Sewing and Alterations: page 73
- Hobbies and Games: pages 163
- An Office: pages 142–143
- A Factory: page 146
- U.S. Mail: page 96; Personal Information: page 4
- Colors: page 12

Part 1

Exercises C & D: Ask questions about quantities of classroom objects. For example:
There are 15 books. There are 22 students in the class. How many more books do we need? Invite learners to create and solve other problems related to classroom objects.

Exercise E: Explain the following rules for adding *-ing:*

1. Add *-ing* to most verbs.
2. For verbs that end with a consonant + *e*, drop the *e* and then add *-ing.*
3. For verbs that end in a consonant + vowel + consonant pattern, double the final consonant and then add *-ing.*
4. If the final consonant is *w, x,* or *y*, follow rule 1. Also follow rule 1 if the last syllable is not stressed.

Part 2

Expressing Time: Introduce and explain A.M. and P.M. prior to reading Part 2.

Exercises A & B: Review differences in third-person-singular verb form in Exercise A and first-person-singular form in Exercise B. Also point out use of the infinitive form in the example questions that follow each exercise.

Part 3

Total Physical Response: Use TPR techniques to introduce and practice packing and shipping instructions.

Draw and Write: Ask learners to design a sweater on graph paper.

Dictation: Dictate simple statements. Learners can write the entire sentence or just the item numbers, sizes, and colors. For example: *I want a red sweater, size medium. I like style number 3324A.*

Songs: You might enjoy teaching "New York, New York" or "California, Here I Come."

Chapter 3 — Perecles Pappous [Per i clēz Pä poos]

Related Topics from *The Oxford Picture Dictionary:*

- School: pages 5, 112
- The Legal System: page 99
- Job Search: page 141
- The Calendar: page 18
- Time: page 16

Part 1

Exercises C-E: Ask questions about Perry's past and present jobs. Help learners talk about jobs they have had and would like in the future. For example: *What was Perry's job in the restaurant? Where did Perry work as an Inventory Control Manager? What job would you like?* Help learners identify important information in the want ads in Exercise C: job titles, workplaces, addresses and telephone numbers. Discuss how to apply for each of the jobs in the ads.

Part 2

Exercises A & B: Review the meanings of A.M. and P.M., and point out that these abbreviations can be used interchangeably with their counterparts. As learners talk about Perry's and their own appointments, point out the irregular present tense verb forms: *have/has.*

Part 3

Exercises C & D: These activities provide learners with opportunities to take leadership roles.

Brainstorming: Ask learners to suggest different topics for discussion at staff meetings in a workplace, such as a school, medical clinic, store, or restaurant. List ideas on the board or on chart paper. Encourage learners to talk about any meetings they have attended.

Additional Discussion: Ask questions such as: *Are American laws the same as laws in (your native country)? What other problems can lawyers help people with?*

Dictation: Dictate simple statements. Learners can write the entire sentence or just the day and time. For example: *There's a meeting on Monday afternoon at 3:00.*

Song: You might enjoy teaching "Nine to Five."

Chapter 4 — Lee Mei Bik [Lē Mā Bik]

[Note: Lee is Mei Bik's last name, so she should be referred to as Lee Mei Bik or Mei Bik.]

Related Topics from *The Oxford Picture Dictionary:*

- Family: pages 24–25
- Office Work: pages 142–144
- A Bank: page 97
- City, State, ZIP Code: page 4

Part 1

Exercises C & D: Ask questions about places where Mei Bik lived. Locate the places on a map of the U.S. Help learners talk about where they live now and where they have lived in the past.

Reverse Chronological Order: Prepare a flow chart for Mei Bik's story. Have learners identify places in the order they occur in this story. Then explain that on job applications and resumes, the opposite order is used. Introduce the words *current* and *previous.* Help learners talk about their own current and previous addresses.

Draw and Write: Give learners a map of the U.S. and ask them to locate and write about places where they (or relatives) have lived or visited.

Exercise E: Follow up by having learners find examples of contractions in the story. Have learners write their own sentences using the contractions. Alternatively, give a dictation using the contractions in simple sentences about Mei Bik's story.

Part 2

Exercises A & B: Help students arrange words and names in alphabetical order. Point out examples of items arranged in alphabetical order, such as phone books, indices, and dictionaries. If possible, allow learners to use a computer to sort a list of words or names alphabetically.

Part 3

Exercise B: Use TPR techniques to introduce and practice the direction words. For example: Say, *"Add 10 and 20. Subtract 5 from 30."*

Ask learners to look through the instructions on the tax form and circle the direction words and vocabulary from the previous page. Demonstrate and model the task using information about your family or a volunteer's family. If possible, use calculators, adding machines, or computers to perform the operations or to check work. Learners can work in groups or pairs to complete the activity.

Dictation: Dictate simple statements. Learners can write the entire sentence or just the name as it is spelled. For example: *My last name is Garcia: G-A-R-C-I-A.*

Songs: You might enjoy teaching "I Left My Heart in San Francisco" or "Going to the Chapel."

Chapter 5 — Sergio Gonzalez
[Ser jē ō Gon za lez]

Related Topics from *The Oxford Picture Dictionary:*

- Construction: pages 147, 149–151
- School: pages 112–113, 118–121
- Family: pages 24–25
- Transportation: pages 90–91

Part 1

Exercises C & D: Ask questions about going to school and working at the same time. Talk about the G.E.D. and adult education programs. Help learners talk about their preferred work times. For example: *When does Sergio work? Can you work nights? When can you work?*

Advantages/Disadvantages: Ask learners to suggest advantages and disadvantages for full-time/part-time work. Help learners talk about pay, benefits, and hours. Prepare a simple two-column T-chart for learners to complete:

Advantages   Disadvantages

Exercise E: Explain plural ending rules. Contrast words that end with a consonant + *y* with words that end with a vowel + *y*. Help with pronunciation of the extra syllable for the plural ending with nouns that end in *s, sh, x,* and *ch*. Ask learners to look back through Sergio's story for other examples of plural nouns.

Part 2

Calculating Time: As a group, calculate the number of minutes and hours spent in class, at work, etc. Help learners use the preposition *at* to talk about a specific time of day and *for* to talk about a duration of time. Also introduce and explain how *it takes* is used when we talk about lengths of time.

Part 3

Reading Labels: Have learners suggest precautions for using dangerous materials at work or at home. Discuss emergency treatment and practice reporting symptoms.

Follow-up: Discuss appropriate ways to warn others of dangers.

Dictation: Dictate simple statements. Learners can write the entire sentence or just the mode of transportation and the amount of time. For example: *I ride the bus. It takes 30 minutes.*

Song: You might enjoy teaching "Respect."

Chapter 6 — Yenework Alemayehu
[Ye ni work Ä lē mā yoo]

Related Topics from *The Oxford Picture Dictionary:*

- Places to Live: page 34, 36–38
- City Streets: pages 88–91
- Clinics: page 84
- A Hospital: pages 86–87
- A Childcare Center: pages 94–95
- School: page 5

Part 1

Write and Draw: Learners may write about and illustrate an American custom that is different or surprising to them.

Part 2

Follow-up: Help learners talk about other places that offer assistance. Role play calling for information about services.

Part 3

Total Physical Response: Use TPR techniques to introduce and practice the parenting skill instructions.

Follow-up: Have learners discuss techniques for dealing with angry customers, co-workers, neighbors, or family members. Learners can role play situations and discuss alternative ways of dealing with each of the situations.

Dictation: Dictate simple statements. Learners can write the entire sentence or just the place/agency and the phone number. For example: *Call the hospital. The phone number is 555-1330.*

Song: You might enjoy teaching "The Children" from *The King and I.*

Chapter-Specific Teaching Notes